# ProBlogger

# ProBlogger

## Secrets for Blogging Your Way to a Six-Figure Income

**SECOND EDITION**

Darren Rowse
and
Chris Garrett

Wiley Publishing, Inc.

ProBlogger: Secrets for Blogging Your Way to a Six-Figure Income, Second Edition

Published by
**Wiley Publishing, Inc.**
10475 Crosspoint Boulevard
Indianapolis, IN 46256
www.wiley.com

Copyright © 2010 by Wiley Publishing, Inc., Indianapolis, Indiana

Published by Wiley Publishing, Inc., Indianapolis, Indiana

Published simultaneously in Canada

ISBN: 978-0-470-61634-5

Manufactured in the United States of America

10 9 8 7 6 5 4 3 2 1

**Library of Congress Control Number:** 2010922559

*Dedicated to our families, friends, and the bloggers we have yet to meet.*

# Credits

**Acquisitions Editor**
Scott Meyers

**Project Editor**
Sydney Jones

**Senior Production Editor**
Debra Banninger

**Editorial Director**
Robyn B. Siesky

**Editorial Manager**
Mary Beth Wakefield

**Marketing Manager**
David Mayhew

**Production Manager**
Tim Tate

**Vice President and
Executive Group Publisher**
Richard Swadley

**Vice President and
Executive Publisher**
Barry Pruett

**Associate Publisher**
Jim Minatel

**Project Coordinator, Cover**
Lynsey Stanford

**Compositor**
Chris Gillespie,
Happenstance Type-O-Rama

**Proofreader**
Nancy Carrasco

**Indexer**
Robert Swanson

**Cover Image**
© porcorex/istockphoto

**Cover Designer**
Michael E. Trent

# About the Authors

**Darren Rowse** is the guy behind ProBlogger.net, which has become one of the leading places on the Web for information about making money from blogs. He is a full-time blogger himself, making a six-figure income from blogging

The authors Darren Rowse (right) and Chris Garrett (left).

now, since 2005. In addition to his blogging at ProBlogger, Darren also edits the popular Digital Photography School (http://digital-photography-school.com), as well as Twitip Twitter Tips (http://www.twitip.com).

Darren lives in Melbourne, Australia with his wife, Vanessa, and sons, Xavier and Henri. In his spare time, he's a mad photographer and has an interest in emerging forms of church and spirituality.

**Chris Garrett** is a writer, Internet marketing consultant, and, of course, professional blogger. As well as his own blog, chrisg.com, he runs an online training class called the Authority Blogger Course (http://AuthorityBlogger.com) and writes for many sites, including CopyBlogger, and occasionally a blog you might have heard of called ProBlogger. He lives in the U.K. with his wife, Clare, his daughter Amy, his dog, Benji, and his grumpy old cat, Tigger. Chris is still trying to move his family back to Canada, if any readers happen to carry a magic wand. When he is not at the computer (rare) you can bet he is out taking mediocre pictures with his digital camera.

# Acknowledgments

From Darren Rowse — A blogger is only ever as good as those around them. I dedicate this book to those in my life who make me better at what I do and who I am. To my family, especially Vanessa, who encouraged me to pursue this "crazy blogging thing;" and to the readers of ProBlogger, who have taught me so much about blogging.

From Chris Garrett — Thanks to my family for supporting me with love and cake, my smart chrisg.com readers, my lovely customers, and to the great folks at Wiley for helping us get to the end with (most of) our sanity intact.

Finally, thanks to the following readers who supplied feedback for this edition:

Jonathan Thomas (http://www.anglotopia.net)

Sean Ashcroft (www.stickyclients.co.uk)

Nadja Specht (www.nuvota.com)

Cathy Stucker (http://BloggerLinkUp.com/)

Chris D. (http://www.ChrisD.ca)

Paul Cunningham (http://www.bloggingteacher.com)

Andrew Mudaliar (www.bargaincity.ca)

# Contents

# Introduction

## Becoming a ProBlogger: Darren's Story of Blogging

During the first year of my blogging career, I worked three jobs simultaneously, studied part-time, and blogged on the side.

A common misconception that first-time readers arriving at ProBlogger.net have is that the six-figure income I've earned from blogging was something that I achieved overnight. It wasn't.

Though blogging has enabled a growing number of people to earn an income, the process is rarely a quick one. For this reason I'd like to share my own story of blogging — from hobbyist to full-time blogger.

So, grab a coffee, make yourself comfortable, and relax — this could take a little while.

### Once Upon a Time...

In November, 2002, when I first hit "Publish" on my original (and short-lived) blog, I did so believing that this "blogging thing," which I'd only just heard of that day, would be nothing more than a bit of fun.

I started this blog for a number of reasons, but it was largely out of curiosity, the idea of having a new hobby, and the hope that perhaps I might meet some new people with similar interests to mine.

At the time I was working three jobs.

### My Three Jobs

My main job at the time was as a minister of a church, three days per week. It was a part-time job (I was not "the" minister but one of four working in a team), and my responsibility was to work with young people.

I was engaged to be married (to Vanessa, or "V," as I call her) and trying to save for a wedding and pay off a car loan and college fees, so I had also taken on a number of part-time jobs (minister's wages are not fantastic at the best of times, but part-time they are even less spectacular).

My second job was working for an online department store. Although that might sound interesting and useful for what was to come in blogging, it was not. I was the warehouse "dog's-body," and my job consisted largely of sweeping, cleaning, lifting boxes, packing orders, and other menial and boring tasks. Still, it helped pay the rent.

My third job was as a casual laborer. I was on-call with an employment agency and did all kinds of temping work ranging from mind-numbing production-line work on a conveyor belt to helping to assemble circuses (don't ask).

Alongside these jobs I was finishing off my theology degree part-time — a long-term endeavor which took 10 years to complete.

This was my life that fateful day when I first got the taste for blogging.

## Hobby Blogger

I'd like to say that at the moment I hit "Publish" on my first blog that the earth shook and a light from heaven came down and I was suddenly transformed into a full-time blogger — but as we all know, it usually doesn't happen that way, and it didn't for me.

In fact, for the first 12 or so months of my blogging very little changed. If anything, I became busier as a result of taking on an extra subject at college and leaving my job as a minister to lead a team starting a new, "emerging church."

Blogging at this time was a hobby and a way to connect with others who were thinking through issues of the "emerging church."

My blog LivingRoom (www.livingroom.org.au/blog) became reasonably popular in emerging-church circles that year, and my site-hosting and ISP costs (I was still on dial-up) began to escalate.

It was after about a year of blogging that I accidentally started Digital Photography Blog; it was originally a photoblog, but no one looked at my images, and the review that I wrote of my camera got a lot of traffic. In an attempt to help cover my hosting costs, I decided to add some AdSense ads and the Amazon Affiliate program to this blog. I just wanted to cover expenses.

I quickly discovered that my hope of covering my costs was realistic, not simply because of AdSense, but also because I put it on an established blog that was getting several thousand readers per day (this is important to keep in mind).

Even with established traffic the earnings in the early days were not high. In my first month (October, 2003), I averaged about $1.40 per day, and that was with lots of curiosity clicks from my readers; by November, I'd hit $3 a day.

The money was minimal, but it covered my costs, and I began to wonder if with the extra few dollars a month I might be able to save up for a new computer (up to this point I was blogging on dial-up from a six-year-old PC that worked most days). My other lofty goal was to save for a professional blog design.

December saw daily earnings hit $6 per day, January $9, February $10, and March $15 — hardly big dollars, but I began to wonder what would happen if I saw the same sorts of increases in income over a longer period of time. By that I don't mean adding $2 to $3 to the daily average per month, but what would happen if I could sustain 30-, 40-, or even 50-percent growth each month?

I began to think in terms of exponential growth.

## Part-Time Blogger

Around this time, I had a little more time on my hands and was in need of another part-time job.

My study was winding down (I finally graduated), and other jobs ended. "V" (my wife by now) began to hint that maybe I should start looking for another part-time job (rightfully so), and we decided that when I finished my degree at the end of June, I'd need to get serious about finding another two days of work per week. All this time I was secretly doing the calculations in my mind to see how much I'd need to earn per day to be able to call blogging my part-time job.

April's earnings came in and averaged around $20 per day, and I realized that I just might have myself a part-time job already. The beauty of blogging income is that it earns you money seven days per week, so I totaled $140 per week.

I began to work harder (largely after hours and late into the night), with the hope of getting earnings up high enough to convince "V" to let me pass on getting a "real" part-time job and to concentrate on blogging.

The work paid off: In May earnings hit $32 per day, and by the end of June, I'd broken $1,000 in a month for the first time and was bringing in $48 per day.

It was crunch-time, and "V" and I had to consider our next move. I could probably keep growing things each month by working after hours on blogging and go find another job — or I could put the two free days that had been taken up by study into blogging and see if I could make a go of it.

I decided to put six more months of effort into blogging to see where it would end up. At the end of the six months, "V" and I would assess the situation again — the threat of getting a "real job" still loomed. I also got my new computer and the professional blog design that I'd been eyeing.

I'll pause here in my story to say that this was a bit of a freaky moment for both "V" and me. Neither of us had started a small business, and though I've always had something of an entrepreneurial spirit, we are both fairly conservative people in many ways. Although the figures indicated that there was potential on many other levels, it just seemed plain weird.

I mean, who makes their income blogging? Needless to say, we didn't tell many people of our decision, and when we did tell a few family and friends, there were plenty of raised eyebrows and lots of comments like, "That's nice, but are you going to get a real job?" and, "How's your little hobby business going?"

I'll stop going into the monthly earnings at this point except to say that investing the two days per week into blogging proved to be one of the best decisions we made. I will stress that this decision came after I'd already been blogging for 19 months and after establishing a number of blogs that were earning reasonable money.

Quitting jobs is not something I recommend people just do off-the-cuff in their early days of blogging. Work up over time, because though it worked out for me, there are plenty of others for whom it has taken a lot longer, and some for whom it just hasn't worked at all.

Throughout the second half of 2004, I continued to put two days per week into blogging while maintaining another three days a week of other work (some church work and some warehousing). It was more than two days per week in practice because I continued to work long hours in the evenings to keep things moving forward, and at times worked literally around the clock (like during the Olympics when I partnered with another blogger to run a blog on the games).

This was a time when I began numerous blogs (I had 20 at one point) and experimented with many different income streams and advertising systems. It was during this time that I also started blogging seriously about blogging and had an active blog-tips section on my LivingRoom blog. This didn't go down too well with some of my readers there, and so I decided to move all of those tips to a new blog called ProBlogger.net. It launched on September 23, 2004.

## Full-Time Blogger — Eventually

By mid December of 2004 we had pretty much decided that 2005 would see me go full-time as a blogger. I'd already ditched most of my warehousing work because the earnings from blogging had continued to rise, and my paid church work had ended as we transitioned the church to a voluntary leadership model.

All was going well, with some amazing figures in terms of earnings in November and December, until what felt a little like disaster happened in mid December. Google did one of its notorious updates where some bloggers go way up in search results and others go way down — I was in the latter group and most of my blogs virtually disappeared from Google, taking with them almost three-quarters of my traffic and earnings. Ouch!

Things looked a little uncertain for the first time in more than six months, and I wondered if the next Google update would see things back to where they were or get worse. The Google update in mid December left us at a level where we could still get by, but it was time for a contingency plan. I even went out and got another part-time job for a while.

The next Google update brought things back to a level just under what they were before. The experience did teach me many lessons, including the importance of diversifying your interests, not relying only on search-engine traffic, and expecting the unexpected when working online.

2005 was a massive year. I worked the part-time job that I'd got during the "Google crash" and worked full-time on my blogging (a juggling act, but both were worthwhile). I continued to diversify my efforts, which resulted in new blogs and partnerships, including developing a course called Six Figure Blogging with another blogger, Andy Wibbels. The name for the course came as I realized that I'd in fact grown my blogging to a point where I earned more than $100,000 per year from the medium — a staggering realization.

Since 2005 the business has continued to evolve with a number of developments including:

- **Starting a blog network — b5media — with a small group of other bloggers —** b5media began as a handful of blogs networked together but grew to be over 300 blogs which employed hundreds of blogs from around the world. The business took on $2 million of venture-capital investment in 2006 and has continued to grow.
- **Launching of TwiTip.com —** With the rise in Twitter I saw an opportunity to create a Twitter Tips blog.
- **Moving into ebook publishing —** As I saw the economy begin to decline in 2008 I started making plans for diversifying my income by selling products of my own. In 2009, I launched two ebooks from my main two blogs: "31 Days to Build a Better Blog" and "The Essential Portrait Guide." In 2010, I launched a second photography ebook called "Photo Nuts and Bolts." Numerous other e-books are currently in production.
- **ProBlogger community —** As another diversification move, I started ProBlogger.com, a community companion site for ProBlogger.net. This paid membership site has grown to well over 2000 members and is a place where bloggers gather to take the principles taught on the free blog further.

## Lessons from My Journey

So why am I telling this story? Is it just a self-gratification thing? I have enjoyed reminiscing, but there's more to it than that. The main reason I wanted to tell the story is because I think it's important to keep emphasizing a number of points:

1. **Blogging for an income takes time.** Although there are stories of people making good money from blogs faster than I have (I've been at it since 2002, remember), there are many others whose growth has been slower. I've had my share of luck, have worked insane hours, and I started out at a time when blogging was a lot less competitive than it is now. All of these things have contributed to my success. It took me more than 1.5 years to be able to call blogging a part-time job, and another year before I went full-time. Building up to going pro as a blogger takes time.

2. **Take it one step at a time.** Unless you have a massive pile of cash somewhere or a sugar daddy (or mommy) to cover your expenses, you need
   to approach blogging professionally one step at a time. My approach
   was to always have a backup plan and to increase the time I dedicated
   to blogging only gradually as it started to show me earnings that justi-
   fied it. My wife and I decided what level of income I needed to earn and
   agreed that as long as blogging was bringing in less than that, I would
   need other work. We put a time limit on it. If income hadn't reached
   the level we wanted within that time frame, I would have been looking
   for work. Though this might sound a little rigid or a bit of a downer,
   I didn't want to run off ahead of "V" in my own direction without our
   decisions being joint ones that we were both comfortable with. "V" has
   been incredibly supportive in all this and has allowed me to follow my
   dreams even when they seemed quite bizarre — but there have also been
   times when she's rightly been the voice of reason and pulled me back
   to earth.

3. **It takes hard work and discipline.** As I mentioned a number of times in
   this story, there have been countless nights when I've worked into the
   wee hours of the morning blogging. Though I have better boundaries
   these days, it wasn't unusual for me to post 50 times per day over 12
   hours in front of the screen. I love blogging, so this isn't a chore all of
   the time, but I'd be lying if I said there weren't days (and weeks) that I
   didn't want to slack off and ignore my business. Friends talking about
   starting a home-based business often say to me that they'd never be able
   to do it because they'd be too tempted to never work. I always thought
   I'd be like this too, but I've worked hard at being disciplined and working hard, and I credit a lot of my success to that discipline.

4. **Follow your dreams.** The main point of this story was to communicate
   the preceding three points and to give a realistic view of the process of
   becoming a pro blogger. I never want to be accused of giving an unbal-
   anced view of blogging or hyping it up as a get-rich-quick thing.

Having said all this, it would also be irresponsible of me not to say that it is
possible to make money blogging — and for some (but not all), it is possible
to make very good money doing it.

There is a growing number of bloggers earning a full-time living from
blogging (we employ a few at b5media) and even more that supplement their

income on a part-time basis while spending other time doing other work, raising a family, or studying.

My hope is that this book will help the number of people making a living from blogging increase even further.

## Chris Garrett's Blogging Story

My blogging story is quite different than Darren's and, in fact, Darren plays quite a pivotal role in it.

The early part of my career consisted of various IT and programming roles until I discovered the Internet or, more accurately, the Internet found me!

I was working for a college in the U.K. when the management decided we should have Internet infrastructure and a website. The task for setting all this up fell to me.

Although I had experienced the Internet in a limited way, and had been online for a while, first through "bulletin boards" then later using Usenet discussion groups, it was my first experience of the Mosaic web browser that switched me on to the Internet in a real way, and this project meant learning everything, and in detail. I was hooked from that moment.

As well as the college website, I built my own, one after another. I had a science-fiction news site, I built sites around my favorite Usenet newsgroups, and, of course, I had a personal homepage. Then I started doing sites on the side for local companies.

After that I took various Web and marketing-agency roles and looked for ways to increase my connections and job marketability. This, combined with a naturally helpful nature, and also being a complete geek, meant that I was active on discussion lists and forums. Getting known in those geek communities led to writing work, which led to co-authoring a couple of programming books, which led to even more of a geek profile.

Around this time I started trying to supplement my meager salary with building affiliate marketing websites. Though I had some successes hawking magazine subscriptions, lawyer leads, and loans, my heart really wasn't in it. My programming websites still did very well, bringing in leads for my programmer-training sideline and freelance writing.

It was Darren and Google AdSense that switched me on to professional blogging.

Though I had hand-developed a blog as a journal in 1999, in fact before they were called "blogs," and routinely blogged and wrote articles about programming, it was the knowledge that you could make money off blogs *without* selling products you don't necessarily have an interest in that made me a true believer.

I fell out with AdSense almost as quickly as I fell in, but thanks to Darren I knew this blogging thing was a perfect fit for me.

My biggest blogging achievement to date is probably having worked on Performancing.com before it was sold to Splashpress Media. I was one of the founding bloggers on the site. In the space of a year we took it from nothing to number 15 on the Technorati 100 list, had our software downloaded hundreds of thousands of times, and had more than 30,000 registered users.

Fast-forward a few years to today; I now make 100 percent of my income from blogging. Unlike Darren, all my income is generated *because* I blog rather than *from* my blogs necessarily.

Rather than sell advertising space or use Google AdSense, my income is from selling consultancy, running online courses such as my Authority Blogger Course and selling ebooks, both my own and as an affiliate for products I highly recommend.

# Blogging
# for Money

It is hard to miss the word "blog" today. We hear blogs mentioned in the media, see them all over the World Wide Web, and we even hear them discussed now in business and social situations. In many cases the term "blogger" is used not just to describe a person who writes a blog, but also someone who earns money doing it.

In this chapter we examine what blogging actually is and what it involves; we then examine the different types of bloggers, and the truth about making money blogging.

Before we get into earning money from a blog, we had better define what exactly a blog is.

## What Is a Blog?

So what exactly is a blog? Because we are at the beginning of a blogging book, this is definitely an issue we need to be clear on!

There are a number of ways we can answer this question, ranging from the broad to the highly technical. To put it as clearly as possible, *a blog is a particular type of website*. You can see an example in Figure 1-1.

Studies have shown that although awareness of blogs is increasing, many people frequent blogs without realizing it. This is fine; the key thing is that readers get value out of it. Anyone who has been reading blogs for a while, though, will know there is more to blogging than just publishing any old website.

Though blogs started out as informal lists of links and personal journals, they have evolved into a far more varied medium. In addition to diary blogs and link blogs, there are now CEO blogs, educational blogs, marketing blogs — you name it!

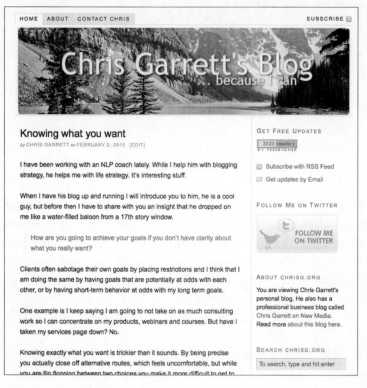

**Figure 1-1:** A typical blog.

Even blogs on a seemingly similar topic can be approached very differently. Just compare chrisg.com and ProBlogger.net, the blogs belonging to the authors of this book. You can see that although blogs have a lot of features in common, they can also be implemented with your own individual style.

## What Makes Blogs Different?

If blogs are just websites, what makes them so different?

In my opinion there are three main areas that differentiate a blog from any other type of site:

 **Content** — Blogs are usually updated more often than traditional websites are; many are updated multiple times a day, and this keeps visitors coming back more often. The content is also normally arranged in reverse-chronological order with the most recent "post" (article) at the top of the main page and the older entries toward the bottom.

- **Syndication** — Not only can blog followers read a blog in their web browser just like they can any other website, a blog almost certainly provides the content in the form of a "feed." In other words, the articles posted to the site are provided in a machine-readable format, allowing people with the appropriate software to read the blog posts as they are published without actually visiting the site.
- **Conversation** — The style of a blog is quite different from other types of websites; there is more of a conversational and community feel. Unlike a purely informational site, or a traditional news site, blogs are written with the bloggers communicating directly to their audience, and replies are expected in the form of comments. In addition to the conversation happening on each blog, conversation also happens between blogs, with one blog post attracting replies and responses on others.

### EXERCISE

The best way to really get a feel for what makes blogs so special is to go out and read a few.

Find as many interesting blogs as you can and note the following:

1. What appeals to you?
2. What does not appeal to you?
3. What sort of content do the blogs you looked at provide?
4. How often do they update?
5. What sort of reader reaction do they get?

When you find a couple of blogs that you enjoy reading regularly, you will begin to appreciate the subtle differences in style and approach to other forms of web publishing. You might also appreciate the pleasure blogs provide over and above their potential to generate financial gain!

## The Added Benefits of Blogging

Yes, blogging has many benefits. Although many bloggers get pleasure just from the process of writing, and of course we cannot overlook the bloggers who make money, blogging may help you achieve other goals:

- **Fame** — A successful blog has the potential to get you noticed and help you build a more visible profile in your business market, pastime, or community.

- **Contacts** — Blogs are excellent ways to get to know people and network. Because blogs naturally lead to conversation, a well-read blog will put you in contact with a wide variety of people.
- **Traffic** — Attracting highly targeted visitors alone could be a big draw, especially if you have products or services to sell. Website owners are always looking for new sources of traffic, and blogs are a proven way to generate more visits and increased loyalty.
- **Sales** — In addition to gaining more attention, over time through your articles you can generate trust and build credibility, critical to making sales.

I love blogging. It is great to be able to work from home, on my own schedule, while helping and meeting so many people. I can't imagine a better way to earn a living!

## Making Money with Blogs

We've already mentioned a couple of times that blogs can make you money, but so far we have offered no explanation of how that is the case. This section takes a look at how bloggers make money. While you read this, you may want to think about tactics that appeal to you.

### Introduction to Professional Blogging

Over the past few years blogging has changed a great deal and evolved in many ways. What was once an activity limited to a very small number of people has now exploded into a mini-industry. As the number of bloggers has exploded, so has the number of tools and services available for bloggers.

Online activities that once involved a good deal of perseverance and a lot of technical proficiency can now be quickly and easily performed by anyone with a few clicks and some typing. Web publishing has arrived for the masses.

With these developments and a growing awareness, some individuals have succeeded in profiting from their blogs. In the beginning it was almost unheard of for someone to earn money from their blog; in fact, for many, profit was seen as counter to blogging culture. This soon changed. As the first pioneers shared their income achievements the focus upon making money from blogging has increased. Now, although financial gain might not be expected, it is certainly much more accepted.

Over recent years the term "professional blogger" arrived to describe anyone who approaches blogging not as simply a hobby, but as a professional money-earning activity.

## How Much Could You Earn?

It should be stressed before we go any further that bloggers need to enter into an examination of this topic with realistic expectations. While millions of bloggers are experimenting with professional blogging, most bloggers are not getting rich and are only supplementing their income by blogging.

Although some bloggers like Darren and I do make a full-time living from blogging, and there are bloggers who make way more than either of us do, many more bloggers use their blogging income to subsidize gadget purchases or to offset some Internet costs.

Just like in most walks of life, those who succeed are the few who put in the effort to make a go of it over the long haul, whereas most others fall by the wayside before they really get going.

## Pro Blogging Is Not a Get-Rich-Quick Tactic

It sometimes disappoints people when we tell them to look elsewhere if they want instant riches. Unfortunately for the impatient, it takes time to build a profitable blog. You do not just become a professional blogger overnight any more than you instantly become a professional golfer. If only this was the case! Although blogging involves you making a decision that you are going to earn money from blogging, it is also something you have to work toward over time.

Yes, you *could* make a lot of money from blogging. Read the stories that are going around on blogs of people making decent full-time incomes from blogging and you will get an idea of the sort of earning potential that exists. Take care also to read about and investigate the hard work and time investment required by bloggers who have created a financially viable blog. Remember that for every well-publicized success story you do read about, there are plenty of others around who have tried and failed that you do not read about. There are a lot more people who struggle to make any more than a few dollars from their blogs than who earn those headline-making five-figures-a-month totals.

Don't get us wrong; we aren't not saying this to dampen the excitement and dreams of pro bloggers! The whole point of this book is to help you achieve exactly those dreams, but we think it is the responsibility of those of us who are "talking up" blogging to also keep giving reality checks. There are no magic wands, no hidden tricks, and no secret handshakes that can bring you immediate success, but with time, energy, and determination you can get there.

## Direct and Indirect Earning Methods

We go into more detail about exactly how you can earn money from a blog later in this book, but making money from blogging is achieved with two broad categories of tactics: *direct* and *indirect* monetization.

Most blogs and bloggers tend to use one or the other of these methods, but there is nothing to stop bloggers from experimenting with elements of both.

### Direct Monetization

Direct methods include strategies that enable bloggers to earn an income directly *from* their blogs. Examples include the following:

- Advertising
- Sponsorships
- Affiliate commissions
- Paid reviews (If you are caught by Google selling links you can lose your rankings.)

As you can see in Figure 1-2, Darren creates revenue directly through displaying advertising.

**Figure 1-2:** Sponsor advertisements on ProBlogger.net.

## Indirect Monetization

Indirect methods include those in which bloggers earn an income *because* of their blog. This could be taking your blog-derived authority, credibility, and expertise and using it for any of the following:

- Freelance contracts
- Books and ebooks
- Speaking engagements
- Consultancy opportunities
- Service contracts
- Running courses, classes, and workshops
- Membership sites and paid communities

When you visit my blog, shown in Figure 1-3, you will not see any ads, but you will see references to my indirect monetization methods.

**Figure 1-3:** Using a blog to sell services.

## Passive and Active Income

A big appeal for making money out of blogs, or in fact web publishing in general, is that many people see it as a passive income or income that is earned even when they are not actively working.

Although there are aspects to blogging that can be seen as allowing a passive income — for example, advertising can earn you money while you are asleep, you can take days off, and so on — in actual fact you do need to keep working at it to make a steady or increasing income.

Blogs that stay still, do not get cared for, or are obviously built with automated or ripped-off content ultimately decline and disappear. When a blog attracts no visitors, the blogger will not earn income.

## Is Pro Blogging Right for You?

Darren and I speak to bloggers every day who have heard the stories of blogs that make big money and who want to try to make an income from blogging. One of the pieces of advice that we offer, knowing full well that it doesn't always get through, is that it is worth taking time out to ask yourself whether making money with a blog is right for you.

Although this might seem to be a silly or even insulting question to some, it is meant to help you examine your intentions. Not every blogger is suited to blogging for money.

Many new bloggers find that at first the enthusiasm and ideas come easily, but after the first flush of energy has passed it becomes harder and harder to write every day, let alone keep up with all the other activities required to maintain a blog. When your income depends on keeping it up, you might find some of the feelings of excitement and enjoyment have turned to resentment and blogging has become a chore.

## Which Monetization Method Is Right for You?

It is not always obvious which style of monetization you might want to follow. Each monetization tactic is appropriate to a different style of blog and blogger.

Consider the following approaches to blogging and see if they fit you. We have noted which category they *primarily* fall under.

## *Indirect*

Here are some common reasons for blogging that fall in the indirect monetization category:

- You blog to help promote your business.
- You blog because you want to sell your products.
- You blog because you want to promote your writing.
- You blog because you want to make yourself known.

## *Direct*

Here are some common reasons for blogging that fall in the direct monetization category:

- You blog for recreational purposes, about your interests and hobbies.
- You blog to make money in your spare time.
- You blog about products and write reviews.

Now, there is nothing wrong with blogging for more than one reason and a mix of strategies is certainly possible, but bloggers considering adding income streams to their blogs need to be aware of the possibility that the implications of going in that direction might impact their other goals.

Let me share some scenarios of real cases that Darren and I have come across where putting ads on a blog wasn't a good idea. Although they might seem specific, I am sure they represent the story of many bloggers and that you can imagine many more scenarios.

### BUSINESS BLOGS ADVERTISING FOR COMPETITORS

Many entrepreneurs hate the thought of leaving money on the table, so when they hear about blog advertising they think they have found a way to make money from wasted traffic. In fact, what tends to happen is that the ads that are served up by their blogs are for other competing businesses in their field. Although they could block some of the ads, most often more ads come in to replace them. If you are promoting your own products or services, be extremely careful about displaying banners or any offers other than your own. In many cases the space you give over to advertising could be more profitably used to sell your own offering.

### READER UPROAR

One blogger who Darren spoke to told him about the day she added graphical banner ads to her blog that sparked a mutiny among her readers. Previously loyal readers expressed outrage that she'd gone that route. Whereas on some blogs, the readers' sense of ownership is not very high, on other blogs — for one reason or another — readers take great offense when bloggers change the rules midstream, especially when it comes to intrusive or animated banner ads. Depending upon the community levels and the way you introduce the ads, you can end up losing readership when you advertise, and you need to consider whether the benefits of the income ads generate outweigh the disadvantages of loosing readers.

### MONEY OBSESSION

Perhaps one of the saddest examples is of a blogger who had been running a really interesting and reasonably successful blog. Although you wouldn't call him an A-lister, he had a growing and loyal following. Seeing this growth, he got bitten by the "money from blogging" bug so badly that it ended up killing his blog. He deleted from his archive any content that had no income-earning potential and introduced so many ads onto his blog that it was hard to find the actual content. Eventually he ended up writing only on topics that he thought would be earners. By doing so, he lost the vast majority of his readership and ended up with a pretty uninteresting and garish blog.

### DISTRACTIONS AND CLUTTER

A number of bloggers try some advertising and then later pull the ads, largely because the payoff isn't worth giving the space to the ads. Ads contribute an element of clutter to your blog and if the conversion isn't sufficient, using ads can seem quite pointless. Opinions on the usefulness of ads versus the disadvantages of the clutter they create vary from blogger to blogger and sometimes depend on the type of ad chosen and the topic that the blogger is writing about, but it's one of the main reasons we see for bloggers to *remove* advertising.

### LOSS OF REPUTATION

Reputations are increasingly important and very hard to build. It does not take much to lose any trust you have built up. Some bloggers manage to build their reputation, gather an audience, and then wash what they built down the drain. After advertising, many bloggers look to affiliate commissions and paid reviews for their next source of income. The problems start when they consider only the commission value and start promoting affiliate products that they have no knowledge of. Inevitably some of those products will be subpar or even actually rip people off. In promoting defective products or writing inaccurate reviews those bloggers betray their audience, something it is very hard to recover from.

## How to Make Blog Advertising Work for You

Here are the key tips for considering blog advertising:

- Put your reader and content first.
- Don't let ads dominate.
- Ensure only relevant and appropriate ads are displayed.
- Write reviews only for products that you have used.
- Promote affiliate offers only when you are sure they are good value. (Disclose your affiliate relationship so as not to fall foul of the FTC regulations.)

Stick to these tips and you should be fine in most cases.

# Blog Strategies

When they think of earning money from blogging, many people think of only one model:

1. Set up a blog.
2. Make it popular.
3. Earn from advertising.

In fact there are other models to consider.

## Multiple Blogs

First of all there is no reason why you should have only one blog. Darren and I each have several blogs. Although your earnings on an individual blog might not set the world alight, if you have multiple blogs and earn a couple of hundred dollars *per blog*, it could make for quite a nice salary.

## Freelance Blogging

In addition to owning my own blogs, I make a percentage of my income writing for other people. It is enjoyable, can be lucrative, and is actually great marketing for my own blog and me.

Obviously I think it is a good deal for the blogger, but what about the person hiring the blogger? People hire a freelance blogger to blog for them for several reasons:

### Ability

There is the writing itself and then all the other things a blogger needs to do, such as traffic building and promotion, design tweaks, technical stuff like installing plugins and programming, and so on.

### Time

If you are busy running your business but you know you would benefit from a blog, then you might hire someone else to do the actual writing. I know many bloggers who have built up mini-networks of blogs this way without doing much of the actual blogging.

### Network

As you will see later in this book, success can be as dependent on other people as on your own efforts. Sometimes people hire other bloggers who they know are well-connected to gain access to people and communities otherwise out of reach for them.

### Knowledge

At times you might need a subject-matter expert to write on certain topics. Rather than learning it all yourself, you can outsource those articles.

### Credibility

Hiring an already-popular blogger is also an advantage because you can leverage his or her credibility and traffic to boost your own. There's nothing like having a well-known, big-name blogger to drive people to your site.

## Build and Flip

A concept familiar in the real-world real-estate market, building and flipping has transferred over to the virtual world of property development. Essentially it is possible to grow a blog's value and then sell it. You could build from scratch or find an under-developed property, buy it, give it a makeover, and then sell it for a profit.

**EXERCISE**

After reading the preceding sections you will have a good idea of the sort of revenue options that are out there. Take some time to think about which appeal to you and why. Most monetization techniques take a good amount of testing, but knowing in advance where your motivations lie will give you an idea of which strategies you are going to have the energy to persist with.

# Measuring a Blog's Success

If you are building a blog to earn money directly, or if you are hoping to make sales from your blog, then money is your obvious metric to determine how well you are doing. What if direct income or sales leads are not part of your plan? How can you measure the success of your blog then?

Every blogger you speak to seems to have a unique perspective on what determines a successful blog. For some it could be about traffic, others prioritize the number of subscribers, and some bloggers count comments as the best measure. Each metric means different things to different people.

The following sections cover a few measures of success that different bloggers use to evaluate how their blogs are going. Some will be more or less relevant for different blogs and will depend upon the goals and objectives of the blogger.

## Traffic

The most common ways that bloggers use to evaluate a blog are the different measures of traffic. Different bloggers seem to have their own preferences regarding different aspects of traffic, plus each tool you use to measure traffic gives a different result due to the differing methodologies used. It is very rare to find two different tools that agree on any one result, so when measuring traffic it is best to stick to your favorite service and use it to show progress rather than obsessing over the actual numbers. Figure 1-4 shows an example traffic graph for ProBlogger.net.

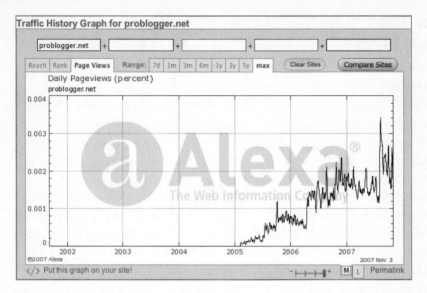

**Figure 1-4:** Alexa graph for ProBlogger.net.

## Unique Visitors

The idea behind tracking unique visitors is to count the number of people who visit your blog. The problem in determining this accurately is there is no way to know who is visiting with any confidence unless you get each person to log in every time they read.

To get a rough idea of how many unique people visit a blog, you can use techniques such as counting each unique IP address (a number given to each device connected to the Internet) or recording "cookies" (small text entries saved by your web browser for later retrieval). All methods have proponents and problems. For example, your IP address today might be different tomorrow, or many different computers could be simultaneously surfing under one number due to differences in how networks are organized. Cookies have a lot of fans, but they are less reliable than they once were because so many people delete them manually or automatically via security and privacy software.

A further complication is that if you have readers who choose to take your content in feed form rather than view your blog in their web browser, your audience is actually larger than this statistic represents.

Advertisers, especially, like to know how many unique visitors your blog attracts in a given month, and if you are going to sell your blog, this metric is extremely important also.

## Visits

An individual visitor could make several visits to a blog. You can measure visits more reliably than you can unique visitors, but to compare results you have to agree on what constitutes a visit.

Visits are also sometimes termed "visitor sessions." Depending on who you listen to and which software you use to measure, a session could be calculated in several ways. One popular way to define a session is as an unbroken stream of page views after a certain period of inactivity. If someone visits two pages ten minutes apart, is that two page views in one session or two visits?

Many website owners take note of average session length as a way to determine how long people spend on their site. As websites become less about downloading pages and focus more on interactivity within a page, session length is gaining attraction. The longer visitors spend looking at your content the better, because it means they were more engaged and according to media-types, gaining more affinity with your brand.

## Page Views

Page views are the total number of pages read in a web browser. Most bloggers like to know how many page views they attract on a daily and a monthly basis.

In addition to the total page views, you should monitor the ratio of pages viewed per visitor. It is best to have a high number of pages viewed and for the average visitor to read more than one page.

Each article you write will receive its own page views, and by comparing individual page counts you can work out which articles are gaining the most attention, giving you an idea what content your audience finds most interesting.

## Hits

Hit counts measure the number of requests sent for a file to the server.

This is a dated and largely unhelpful metric because every request for any file is counted. Although it sounds useful, in actual fact it gives you little actionable information. If you have a page containing four images, one request for that page is counted as five hits. To increase your hits, you can add images to the page!

Due to the misleading nature of the metric, few people use it seriously, and the term *hits* is often incorrectly used in conversation and the media when what they actually mean is to describe traffic in general, or specifically visits or page views.

## Subscribers

Bloggers can vary from being indifferent about subscriber counts to being obsessed with them. Why are subscribers so important?

Counting a blog's subscribers gives a good indication of how popular it really is because subscribers are the people who want to read your content long-term and have signed up to receive updates so they never miss one. These are your loyal readers, the people you can hopefully count on to come back again and again.

Whereas the metrics mentioned before are important, and they are traditional measures for any website, subscribers are critical to blogs. A visit could be a person arriving, not finding what they need, and going away never to return. A subscriber has made a small commitment to you and demonstrates you are providing something useful and compelling.

Subscribers are usually split into RSS subscribers and email subscribers; although, the lines are blurring.

### RSS Subscribers

RSS subscribers are the people who use your feed to read articles. They use a feed reader (service or software application) to pull down updates to your feed and might never actually visit your blog at all.

The most popular feed-measurement service is FeedBurner.com, and because of this, most bloggers rely on that service to compare progress against each other. Both Bloglines and Google provide a count of readers using their feed-reader services, but only FeedBurner provides a count across all of them.

Even though nearly all bloggers rely on FeedBurner, even the company would admit that counting feed readers is not an exact science. Numbers fluctuate every day, and glitches can make it seem like you have lost or gained readers almost randomly. The best idea is to use the count as a progress guide and not an exact count of individuals.

### Email Subscribers

In addition to RSS readers, many bloggers publish their content over email. There are services available to allow you to take your RSS feed and deliver email updates automatically, and then there are specialist email-newsletter-publishing services such as Aweber.com that allow you to create messages or import your content.

An advantage that using email lists has over using RSS is that when a visitor subscribes you get his email address. A list of email addresses is a reliable indicator of how many individuals you have subscribed.

## Comments, Feedback, and Interaction

Much as we all want readers, when a blog is truly engaging you will attract comments. Comments show that your visitors want to interact with you. They allow you to build a sense of community, further encouraging readers to return time and again. You can see an example comment form in Figure 1-5.

**Leave a Reply**

Name (required)

Chris Garrett

Mail (will not be published) (required)

chris@chrisg.com

Website

http://www.chrisg.com/

Great post :)

submit

☑ Notify me of future comments via e-mail

**Figure 1-5:** Writing a comment.

### Comments

You can begin by counting the number of comments you receive after removing junk and spam comments. If on average each article attracts ten comments, you know you have made an improvement over when your blog gained only one or two.

There are two types of posts you might particularly want to receive: good feedback and considered posts. If the only comment you ever receive is, "You suck," you might not be quite as happy about those ten comments as back when you received two "nice post" comments per article!

Many bloggers also judge quality equally as important as quantity because it is so easy to just post any old rubbish into the comment area, and people do just to get a mention of their own website, but when someone takes time and care to craft a thoughtful comment it can be much more satisfying.

### Feedback

Obviously, in addition to comments, people will use your contact form and email to get in touch with you. Many of my best articles have been inspired by reader questions, and it is important to all of us to receive feedback, good and bad, so we know where we are going wrong and what we are doing right.

### Interaction

Beyond comments and emails, there are many ways that readers can participate on a blog. Taking part in your blog might include responses to polls, competition entries, and other calls to action. In general, if people do in large numbers what you ask, then you have an engaged audience!

## Links

Links are the currency of the World Wide Web. The number of incoming links to your blog can be an indicator of how well you are engaging other bloggers. Incoming links are good for a blog in most cases because of the incoming traffic that follows them, but also because they are a major factor in climbing the rankings in search engines.

They can be monitored in a number of ways.

### Trackbacks

If another blogger links to your article you can be notified using a special comment called a Trackback, which appears linking back to the original blogger with a small quote of the text used. Though some bloggers hate them due to spammers taking advantage of the free link back, blogs utilize them to further conversations and as notification of what others are writing about you.

### Search Engines

To find out who is linking to you, type **link:domainname** into Google. You can get a good quick picture of the incoming links that that search engine has indexed for your blog. There are also browser plugins and easy-to-use web services that will show you the same thing.

### Referral Stats

Most statistics packages offer the ability to track where your readers come from to get to your blog. This shows you the things they are searching search engines for but, also the sites that are linking up.

## Search-Engine Results

Getting to the top of a search-engine result for a certain phrase can be the ticket to a flood of traffic and admiration from your peers. Some people take this to the level of a sport, seeing it as a game or competition, whereas other people make an entire career out of it because some search results are worth a great deal of money if you have something valuable to sell. Take a look at Figure 1-6 to see an example search result where Darren ranks top.

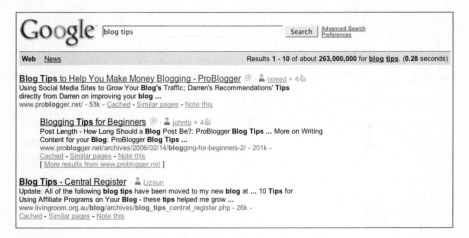

**Figure 1-6:** ProBlogger coming in at the top in an example Google search.

### PROBLOGGER BLOG TIP: USEFUL WEBSITES

The following websites and tools are useful for keeping track of your own progress or comparing one blog to another:

    http://tools.seobook.com/
    www.seomoz.org/tools
    http://alexa.com/

**EXERCISE**

Go back over your list of blogs to read one more time. Do your favorite blogs show any signs of success under the preceding criteria? Do the best have more RSS subscribers, more comments? Can you find them in Google .com and Alexa.com?

**PROBLOGGER BLOG TIP: STAT ADDICTION**

Although monitoring all the statistics mentioned in this chapter can be useful, some bloggers fall into the trap of becoming quite addicted to checking these types of statistics, which can become a pretty competitive and unproductive exercise.

Remember that unlike a lot of endeavors, a blogger doesn't really have competition as such; your fellow bloggers are more normally a source of help, friendship, and traffic rather than adversaries. Plus, it is worth growing a thick skin and keeping your ego in check; sometimes "conversation" can become heated, so keeping a balanced head can be critical!

I, personally, take note of all of these varying degrees of measurements, but it's best not to give them undue attention.

## Summary

In this chapter we examined what a blog is and some of the ways you can use blogging to make money.

Though we do not want you to be pessimistic, we cautioned that it is not something that you will make a ton of money doing overnight, so better hold on to that day job! At the same time it is a great way of earning income, both in terms of the amount of money you can make and the fun you can have doing it.

Over the remainder of this book we go into detail and show exactly how to choose a topic for your blog, what you need to do to build your blog, and how to make it a success.

# 2 Niche Blogging

One of the most important decisions that bloggers wanting to build a profitable blog need to make is what their blog will be about.

In this chapter we introduce you to the concept of *niche blogging* and give you some questions to ask yourself when you are considering what topic to focus your blog upon.

The majority of bloggers starting out in blogging do so by creating a personal blog. These blogs are, in many ways, an extension of the life of the blogger and usually cover a wide array of interests, ranging from life experiences to observations on work, hobbies, relationships, and passions.

Personal blogs can be a lot of fun and are a great place to learn about the basics of blogging; however, having a blog focus upon such a variety of topics and delving into your personal life doesn't always make good business sense.

I started out with a personal blog that covered everything from spirituality and church to photography to blogging (and more), and though the blog did become quite popular, after 18 months of running it, I began to notice a number of things that made me consider a new approach:

- **Some readers became disillusioned with the blog** — My blog had a number of main themes and different readers resonated differently with each one. A few readers shared all of my diverse interests; however, most came to my blog to read about just one aspect of my life. When I focused on a topic they were not interested in, they either ignored the post or, at times, even pushed back. In the end, a number of regular loyal readers became disillusioned with my eclectic approach to blogging and gave up reading me altogether.

- **I began to feel guilty about blogging on certain topics** — Knowing that many of my readers were disillusioned by my scattered approach to blogging, I began to feel more and more guilty about posting on certain topics and began to dread the pushback that I knew I would get when posting on things that I was interested in, but that some readers were sick of reading about. As a result, I posted on topics that I was less interested in to appease readers and ignored other topics that I'd rather have covered.

I found myself in a rather frustrating position; I was the author of a blog whose readers were increasingly complaining and which I enjoyed writing less and less. Something had to change.

After a lot of consideration, I decided to splinter my blog into a number of niche blogs that focused upon specific topics.

This allowed my readers to get the specific information that they wanted and for me to write as much (or as little) on each of those topics as I wanted, knowing that I was writing to people with similar specific interests to mine.

The result was a more natural blogging experience for me and a more useful blog for readers.

## 10 Reasons Why Niche Blogs Are Successful

Although it is not impossible to build a successful blog by blogging on a wide array of topics, the majority of profitable blogs that I've observed target a defined niche.

Look at the top blogs that you read regularly and you'll find that the majority of them have a defined niche. Some niches are wider than others, but in nearly all cases they've carved out a niche for themselves.

There are many reasons why choosing a niche is important for building a successful blog. Let's explore a few of them:

- **Loyal readers** — Niche blogs tend to develop a loyal readership because readers know that when they log into a blog, they'll get relevant information on topics that they have an interest in, rather than random posts on topics that they have no desire to read.
- **Community** — People like to gather with others like them. Many times when you develop a blog focusing on a single topic, you find that a

group of like-minded people will gather around it not just to read what you have to say, but to interact with others who share their passions and interests.

- **Specialist authors** — Authors of niche blogs have the freedom to focus upon a topic without feeling guilty about doing so. This can lead to an increase in the quantity, quality, and depth of articles.
- **Brand, credibility, and profile** — Blogging consistently on one single topic increases the chances of that blog (and its blogger) being seen as a credible, trusted source of information in that area. Work this correctly and you can become the "go-to" person in your niche and become known as a specialist or expert in your field. The flow on benefits of this is huge if you have a product or service of your own to sell. Instead of you needing to go and look for customers, you'll find that people start to seek you out due to your expertise.
- **Contextual advertising** — Contextual ad networks like AdSense tend to work best on sites that are tightly focused. They serve more targeted and relevant ads when a whole site is on a defined topic — which in turn increases the likelihood of those ads being clicked by readers.
- **Ability to sell products** — When you understand a niche well and attract an audience around it, you can create and sell products confident they have an eager market and will be purchased.

## PROBLOGGER BLOG TIP: SPOTTING NICHES

While you are looking around at blogs, try to identify the niche the blogger is working in and unique qualities of that niche. You will find from topic to topic variations in approach and conventions typical to just that niche:

- Overall subject
- Target audience
- Advertiser market
- Related niches
- Successful content types
- Design style
- Tone of voice
- News versus tutorial

By thinking about blog niches this way, your awareness will grow, which will help you develop an eye for potential niches in which you could happily work.

- **Direct advertising sales** — Niche blogs are more attractive to private advertisers or sponsors, who are looking for content to place their ads on that is relevant and closely aligned to their product or service.
- **Search engine optimization** — Google and other search engines tend to favor sites with a well-defined topic with pages that relate to one another.
- **More posts** — I find that I post more if I have five blogs on five topics rather than one blog on five topics. There is only so much you can write on a blog each day without overwhelming your readership.
- **Leverage to expand into neighboring niches** — One benefit of becoming well-known in a highly focused niche is that you can position yourself to springboard into a neighboring or overarching one.
- **Higher conversion** — If your blog's business model is to sell something to your readers, it is to your advantage to have a blog that has a readership with interests that are highly aligned with your own focus. Trying to be all things to all people is a trap that some bloggers fall into. For fear of losing readers, they allow their content to become unfocused and off topic. Though this might help build readership when it comes to selling a product, your conversion rate will be significantly reduced because a lower percentage of readers will be truly interested in your more targeted product. Niche blogging brings in more qualified prospects.

Choosing a niche for your blog enables you, your bloggers, and your readers to become more focused and will enable you to grow a readership and monetize it more effectively.

# How to Choose a Profitable Niche Topic for Your Blog

Defining your niche is important if you want to build a successful blog; but how do you choose one?

Following is a series of questions that we recommend you ask yourself as you make this important decision. We've included some practical exercises with each question to help you tackle them more effectively.

## Are You Interested in the Topic?

A friend of mine recently explained it this way:

"Probably the best place to start thinking about what your blog should be about is to consider what *you* are about."

In other words, start by identifying your own interests, passions, and energy levels for topics. Although it might be tempting to start blogs based on what other people are interested in or what makes commercial sense, there is little logic in starting a blog on a topic that you have no interest in yourself.

There are two main reasons for this.

First, if you want to grow a popular and well-respected blog, it can take considerable time and you'll need to take a long-term approach to building it.

Successful blogs don't happen overnight; as a result, it's well worth asking yourself, "Can I see myself still writing on this topic in a year or two?" If you can't, you might need to reconsider your topic.

The second reason is that your readers will quickly discern whether or not you are passionate about your topic. Blogs that are dry and passionless tend not to grow. Nobody wants to read something that the author doesn't really believe in.

### EXERCISE

Take some time to brainstorm possible topics based solely upon your own passions and interests. What do you know about? What do you do in your spare time? What do you spend your money on? What topic do your conversations with friends always turn to? What ideas or topics keep you awake at night? What books, magazines, TV shows, and websites do you spend time following? Rate each topic in terms of your passion and interest.

## Do You Have Experience or Expertise in the Topic?

This is an important question to consider before you start a blog. Not because you can't start a blog on a topic that you don't have "expert" status in, but because your own experience in the area will determine how you approach the topic.

Take the "make money blogging" niche as an example. I regularly see bloggers starting blogs that claim to teach people how to make money blogging.

They present themselves as experts, but the problem is that many of those behind these blogs have never blogged before and don't have any experience to draw upon when it comes to teaching others how to do what they claim they can teach.

The result is that these bloggers often run out of things to write about. Their readers quickly see through the claims of the bloggers, and the reputation of the blogger is damaged.

A better approach for someone just starting out in a niche with little experience, would be to start up a blog on the topic that is open about what they do and don't know, and that will document their own learning experience on the topic rather than promote a false claim to know it all and be able to teach others.

These blogs can be quite successful because others at a similar stage often gather around them to share the journey of learning with the blogger. Over time these blogs can actually transition into "expert blogs" as the bloggers and their readership grow and become more proficient and experienced in their topic.

> **EXERCISE**
>
> List the topics that you know something about. What have you had training in? What have you had experience in? What topics do people always come to you to find information on? What are you currently learning about or wanting to learn more about? Once you have a list, give each topic a rating in terms of your level of "expertise."

## Is the Topic Popular?

Although the blogger's interest is important, it's not enough to build a popular blog.

Another crucial ingredient is that others *want* to read information on the topic you're writing on.

The law of supply and demand comes into play at this point. You might be interested in your topic and be able to supply great content on it, but unless others are interested in it and are showing demand for it by searching for it, you'll always have an uphill battle in building a well-read blog.

Keep in mind that you are writing in a medium with a global audience of many millions and as a result you don't need a topic that *everyone* is searching, just one that *some* people are searching.

---

**EXERCISE**

Head to a newsagent (newsstand) and take a few minutes to do a little analysis of the array of magazines that you see on display there. What are people into at the moment? Which topics are most prolific when it comes to what people are reading about?

---

## Is the Niche Growing or Shrinking?

The popularity of different topics rises and falls over time.

Ideally you would want to choose a topic when it is on the rise rather than when it is in decline. This is not easy to do, of course, but predict the next big thing that people will be searching for and you could be onto a winner.

Get in the habit of being on the lookout for what people are into. I constantly ask myself, "What will people be searching the Web for in 6 to 12 months, and how can I position myself to be the site that they find when they do?"

Keep an eye on what people are into, what the latest trends are, what events are coming up, and what product launches are on the horizon. Do this online, but also keep an eye on TV, magazines, the papers, and even the conversations you have with friends.

Although it isn't essential to be first to start a blog on a topic, it certainly helps to be early.

---

**EXERCISE**

Go to Google Trends (www.google.com/trends), and type in some of the keywords from niches that you are considering blogging about. Google Trends charts search volumes for different search terms. It tracks only some words (generally popular ones), but it gives a great trend analysis of whether a niche might be growing or shrinking. Compare two or more niches by separating terms with a comma.

## What's the Competition?

One of the traps that some bloggers get sucked into when choosing a topic is to go for the most popular topics with no regard for the competition they might face in those markets.

---

**PROBLOGGER BLOG TIP: NICHE ANALYSIS**

When selecting a niche, you want to determine the audience size, the level of competitiveness, whether there is any money to be made, and how well you can populate your blog with content over the long term.

Although many bloggers say there is no such thing as competition in blogging and that we are all friends, it could be too much of an uphill struggle to try to break into an over-crowded niche when other just-as-effective niches are available.

How much competition is too much? You might be surprised to learn that in some cases you actually *want* competition. There are two reasons why you cannot find many competitors for a particular niche:

1. You are a genius and nobody else has thought of writing about your topic.
2. There just isn't enough interest to sustain a blog long-term.

In most cases it will be the second option, but you can test a niche by creating a new category on your personal blog and seeing what kind of reaction you get.

---

In fact, many bloggers see successful blogs already operating in a niche and decide that if someone else can do it, they should choose exactly the same topic and attempt to emulate them.

A prime example of this is in the gadget blog space where some of the most successful blogs operate (like Gizmodo and Engadget). The problem with starting a blog on gadgets is that there are thousands of other blogs already targeting this niche, with some very entrenched and well-established blogs already taking the lion's share of the market. Though it is not impossible to start a successful blog on gadgets, picking a niche with fewer and less-established competitors might be a wise move.

The chances are that if you have identified a niche that you think is "hot" at the moment, someone else will have also. It's demand and supply coming into play again — for any level of demand for information on a topic, only a certain number of sources of information will be needed on that topic.

The Web is becoming a more and more cluttered place, and sometimes it feels that there are no niches left to blog about. Though this is true in some of the more popular topics, remember that you don't have to go for the topic that absolutely *everyone* is searching for. In fact, sometimes it's some of the less popular topics that have little or no competition that are the best earners.

I have one friend, who after years of attempting to do well writing about gadgets, switched to writing about ride-on lawnmowers (a topic he'd been researching for a purchase he was making). He was amazed to find that after just a couple of months of writing on his new topic, it was garnering significantly more traffic (and making quite a bit more) than his gadget websites ever had.

Sometimes it is better to be a big fish in a small pond rather than a small fish in a big pond.

**EXERCISE**

Head to Google.com and search for blogs on your potential niche. See who has been blogging on your topics. How many other blogs can you find on your potential niche? Make a note of them for the next stage of this process.

## What's the Competition Neglecting?

This question attempts to find "gaps" that are not yet filled in the marketplace. Though your competition might have the advantage of an established audience, you have the advantage of flexibility and can position your blog very quickly to fill a gap in the niche that you might observe. In doing so, you create a sub-niche within the larger topic.

**EXERCISE**

When analyzing your potential competitors you might like to ask some of the following questions:

- What do they do well?
- What are the boundaries of the topics that they focus upon?
- What don't they write about?
- How often do they post?
- How long are their posts?
- At what level are they pitching their blog (beginners, intermediate, advanced)?
- What questions are their readers asking in comments?
- What style or voice do they write in?
- How do they monetize themselves?
- What types of posts seem to get the most attention (comments, Trackbacks, incoming links)?
- What is their design like? What do they do well and what do they do poorly?
- What are other blogs writing about them?
- If they have an open or unlocked stats package what can you learn from their stats? What pages are popular? Where does their incoming traffic come from?

Doing this type of analysis of your competitors will not only help you to work out if there are any gaps that you might fill with your blog, but how you might do it.

The key objective in thinking this way is to develop a blog that is unique and differentiates itself from other blogs.

## Will You Have Enough Content?

One of the key features of successful blogs is that they have the ability to continue to come up with fresh content on their topic for long periods of time.

Conversely, one of the things that kills many blogs is that their authors run out of things to say.

Answering the question regarding whether there is enough content should be done on two levels:

- **Do *you* have enough content within *you* as an author?** This really comes back to the question we asked earlier about your passion, interests, and energy for the topic (so I'll leave it at that).
- **Do you have access to enough other sources of content and inspiration?** There are many Web-based tools around these days that can help you in coming up with content. Some places to check out your topic to see what news is about include Google News, Digg, Popurls (Figure 2-1), StumbleUpon, and Reddit. Do a search for words in your proposed niche and you will quickly see how much is being written about them in mainstream media and on other blogs.

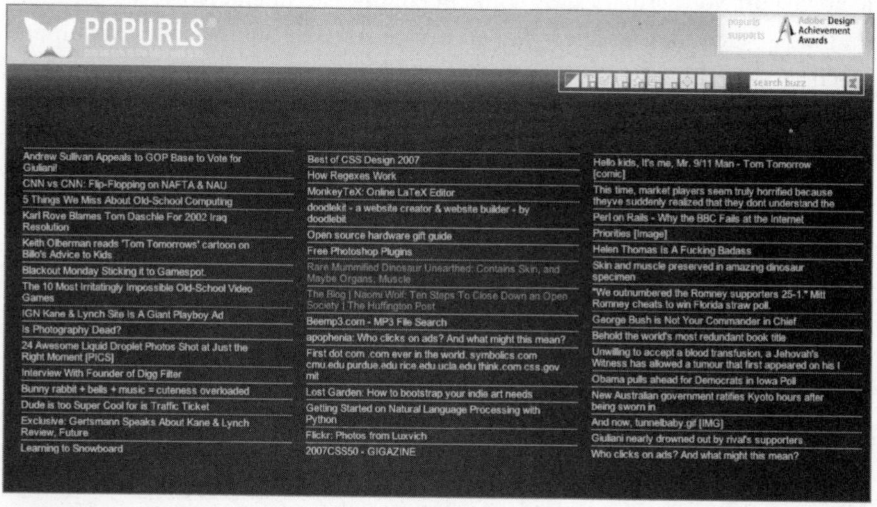

**Figure 2-1:** Popurls links to sources of information.

**EXERCISE**

Set aside an hour to list as many ideas as possible for posts. If you get three minutes into this exercise and have run out of ideas, it could be an indicator that there's not enough content to sustain a blog for the long haul.

# Is the Niche Able to Be Monetized?

If you are interested in earning an income from blogging you will need to factor in some investigation of whether the topic you've chosen has any obvious potential income streams.

There are many ways to earn money from blogs (we introduce you to many of them later); however, the problem is that not every topic is going to be suitable for every potential income stream.

For example, contextual ad programs like AdSense and Chitika work really well for some topics, but earn hardly anything from others. Similarly, some blogs do fantastically out of affiliate programs, some are better suited to selling advertising directly to advertisers, and others are better suited to impression-based ads.

It can be difficult to know how well different income streams will work on a blog before you actually start it and begin to experiment. However, the more digging around and research you do before starting out, the better equipped you'll be to make a decision on which niche topic to choose.

## EXERCISES

- **Look at your competition** — Check out how other blogs and websites in the niche are monetizing their sites. What ad networks are they using? Are they promoting affiliate programs? If the competition has advertiser pages, how much are they charging for them?

- **Search for affiliate programs** — Head to your favorite search engine and type in your potential topic and "affiliate programs." You'll be surprised what will come up when you do this; quite often this will reveal some potential products that you could make some commission on. Try it with a variety of keywords in your search.

- **Search Google** — Do a simple search on Google for the main keywords of your potential niche and see how many ads come up above and down the right-hand side of the search results page. This is an indicator that advertisers are using Google's AdWords advertising program for these keywords. This indicates likelihood that there will be advertisers if you use the Google AdSense program to monetize your blog.

- **Check out Amazon** — Search on Amazon to see if there are related products there that you might be able to link to and make a commission on via their affiliate program.

# How Wide Should a Niche Be?

Blogs come in all shapes and sizes. Take a quick look at some popular blogs and you'll find that some have wide niches. For example, Gizmodo (Figure 2-2) covers news on all kinds of consumer electronics and gadgets — it covers everything from MP3 players to digital cameras, through to GPS devices.

**Figure 2-2:** http://gizmodo.com

Some blogs narrow their niche even further and focus upon just one class of product, or even in extreme cases, one brand or model.

Both wide and narrow niches can work; however, while some analysis of the most popular blogs shows that they quite often have a wide focus, it is also worth knowing that they usually are in quite crowded niches (lots of competition) and take a lot of work to maintain (many of the top blogs have numerous bloggers churning out content for them).

On the flipside, don't choose a niche that is too narrow. I once saw a blog start up on a single model of printer. Though this blog had a well-defined niche, its blogger ran out of things to write about after just a week or two.

The take-home lesson is to choose a niche that you can find enough to write about but that won't overwhelm you.

## Niche Demographic or Niche Topic?

So far we've talked about choosing a niche topic for your blog — something that most successful blogs do.

However, there is another type of niche blog that we're starting to see some bloggers develop — one that doesn't focus upon a niche topic so much as a niche demographic.

These blogs identify an audience that they want to target and then develop content on a variety of topics that would relate strongly to that group of people.

Let me illustrate with a short case study.

## GalaDarling.com

When I first met Gala Darling at a blogger meetup in Melbourne, she described her blog to me as a fashion blog that documented her own tastes and decisions in fashion as well as covering fashion news.

A few months after first meeting Gala we caught up over a coffee to talk blogging and she described her blog (see Figure 2-3) in a slightly different way.

Instead of describing it as a "fashion blog," she spoke about it as a "blog for youthful alternative (unconventional, individual, eccentric) women."

**Figure 2-3:** www.galadarling.com

The way she talked about her blog changed from being one that revolved around a single topic to one that revolved around a certain type of reader or audience.

Fashion still made up a significant proportion of her posts, but so did other aspects of the life of her loyal and growing readership (including travel, relationships, shopping, and music). In a sense Gala is moving toward providing a one-stop shop for her readers rather than just a smaller destination that focuses upon one aspect of their lives.

---

**PROBLOGGER BLOG TIP: THE RIGHT NICHE FOR YOU**

There are two approaches to deciding on your niche: the analytical and the emotional. In most cases our final decision is based on a little of both.

- What type of blog are you drawn to?
- Do you feel excited about working on one topic more than others?
- Are there subjects you just can't stop talking about?
- Do people know you as an "[insert topic here] geek"?

Many of my more successful blogging friends state that if they won the lottery they would still blog; they love their topics so much. Can you think of a subject you could feel that way about?

Remember that professional blogging is hard, takes time, and especially needs lots of valuable and unique content. This is so much easier when blogging a topic you are motivated about.

---

## Choose a Niche

At this point, it's time to choose a topic for your blog. It is highly unlikely that you'll find the perfect topic on all of the fronts discussed earlier.

Although it'd be great to find a topic that you're passionate about that just happens to have massive demand, no competition, and lots of lucrative income streams, the reality is that most topics that you come up with will have at least one weakness to them.

Don't let this get you down; there comes a time when you just need to make a decision and start blogging because the best way to get the answers to many of the questions in this chapter is to start a blog and see what you learn.

The key is being aware of what the weakness is so that you can work to overcome it.

# Tools for Helping You to Choose a Niche for Your Blog

Many tools have been developed that are helpful for bloggers in the process of selecting a niche topic for their blog. The following tools are ones that we use in this research phase:

- **AdWords Keyword Tool** — Sign up as an advertiser with Google AdWords and you get access to a number of useful tools that you can use without actually needing to use AdWords to advertise. One particularly useful tool is the Keyword Tool (`https://adwords.google.com/select/KeywordTool`), which you need to be logged in to use. This allows you to type in a keyword (or phrase) and will give you an indication of how many people searched for that word in the past month as well as tell you how many advertisers are competing for that word in AdWords. This gives you an indication of the popularity of the niche and whether there is potential income in it. This tool will also give you other keywords that relate to the ones you enter, which is also useful to know.
- **Google Trends** — Google has a Trends tool at `www.google.com/trends` (Figure 2-4) that is useful for looking at search volume on Google for different search terms. Though it won't give you specific search numbers and doesn't produce results for every term (it tracks just the most popular ones), it is useful for working out whether a niche is growing or shrinking and it allows you to compare two different terms to show you how big one is in comparison to another.
- **Google Blog Search** — Google's Blog Search will help you to get a picture of who else is blogging on a given topic.
- **Wordtracker** — Wordtracker (Figure 2-5) is a popular keyword-research tool with a free trial that helps you to ascertain how many people are searching for different words and how many other sites are competing in those niches.
- **Yahoo! Buzz** — Yahoo! Buzz (`http://buzz.yahoo.com/`) is a summary of information on what people are searching for at the Yahoo! search engine.

Aaron Wall has also outlined a great list of keyword-researching tools at `www.seobook.com/archives/001013.shtml`. Check it out.

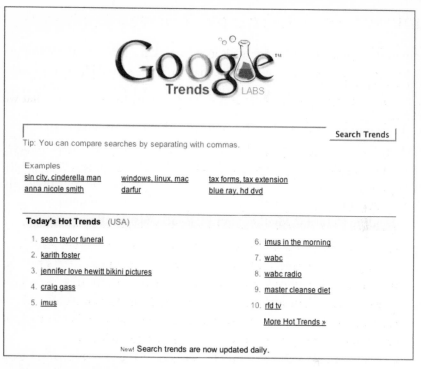

**Figure 2-4:** Google Trends

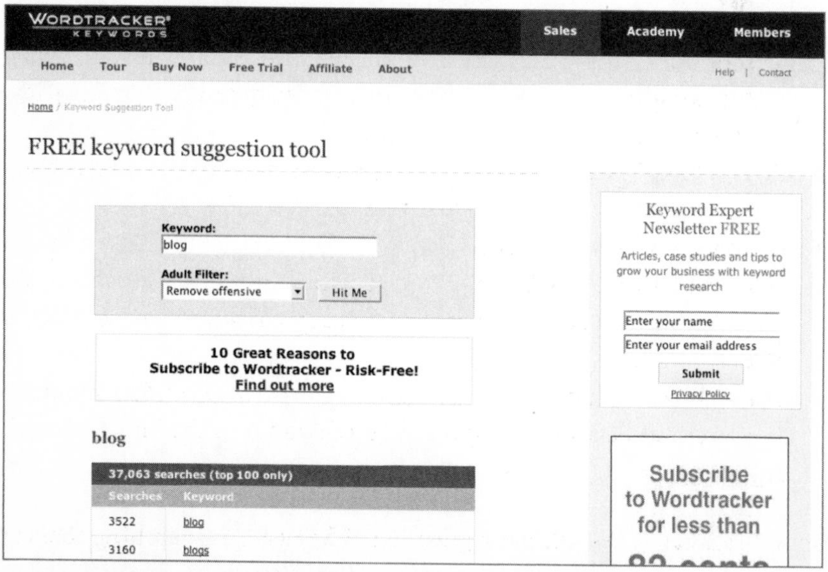

**Figure 2-5:** www.wordtracker.com

## Summary

Although the majority of bloggers choose to go with a personal blog when they first start, we hope we have shown that for professional bloggers, a well-selected niche that you are happy writing for can make all the difference to your earning potential.

In this chapter we looked at the concept of blog niches and gave you an overview of the sorts of considerations that need to be taken into account before selecting your blog topic. What you will write about is a much more important factor than many bloggers realize. The subject of your blog, the audience you aim to attract, and, therefore, the market you go into could well be the deciding factor for whether your blog succeeds or fails.

# 3

# Setting Up Your Blog

So far we have looked at what blogging is and what it means to be a professional blogger, and you have investigated what you might want to write about. We are off to a good start. Before you actually start blogging, though, you will need to set up your blog!

In this chapter, we look at your choices when deciding which blog package to go with, what you need to think about when choosing, and what the most popular combinations are.

After you have decided on what approach you think might suit you best, you need to actually go ahead and set up your blog so it both works and looks great.

With these goals in mind, we go step-by-step through setting up a hosted blog and a self-hosted blog.

## Choosing the Right Blog for You

"Which blog platform should I use?"
"Should I use a free hosted blog or get my own domain?"
"What are the pros and cons of going with one vendor over another?"
"Could I start out on a free blogging service and upgrade later?"

These are just some of the typical questions that we get asked each day from beginner bloggers trying to decide which blogging platform or tool they should choose.

I'm not going to tell you which blog platform you should use because, as you will see, there are good reasons for choosing most of the available platforms, depending upon the goals of your blog and your own technical resources.

Over the years, the choices available to bloggers have grown, while the technicalities involved in blogging have shrunk. This means now more than ever there really are options to suit every potential blogger. It's now so easy that anyone can have a blog working in five minutes flat.

Don't believe it? Just keep reading!

## Blog Platform Choices

As with making any important decision, it is worthwhile to take your time with this decision before jumping in. There are many competing blog platforms on the market, all varying in capability, complexity, price, and popularity. Blogger is one of the most popular platforms with beginners, as shown in Figure 3-1, but because of that people tend to view Blogger blogs as low-quality.

**Figure 3-1:** Blogger is one of the popular blogging platforms for beginners.

Although you can change your blog platform at a later time and many of them do provide ways to move your content, there are usually tricky technical challenges involved and potentially some costs.

Determining which platform suits you is an individual choice, but there are some questions you can answer to make deciding easier.

## What Are Your Goals?

Probably the most important thing to do when starting the process of choosing a blog platform is to consider your aspirations for your blog. Of course, complete first-timers might struggle a little with seeing the future of their blogging, but to the best of your ability, attempt to answer some of these questions:

- Is blogging a passing interest or something you will do long-term?
- What will be the main purpose of your blog?
- Is it for business, or just for personal enjoyment?
- Might you want to show advertisements?

Of course, there are many other questions you'll want to ask, but the answers to these sorts of questions are worth keeping in mind as you research blog platforms. Some services are much more suited to the hobby blogger and others to more professional blogging applications.

## What Is Your Budget?

As with most things in life, blog platforms come with a variety of price points. All hosted platforms offer varying levels of service, and self-installed software varies in price from free to expensive (see Figure 3-2).

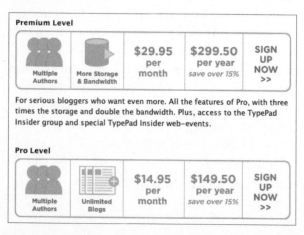

**Figure 3-2:** TypePad service levels.

There are three main things that you might pay for:

- The blog software itself or level of service, one-off or ongoing
- Monthly hosting for your blog
- Your domain name annual renewal fee

There is also potentially an additional cost for custom design and programming depending on your budget and how serious you are. Most people start out with freely available designs and tweak them to suit their own tastes and needs.

Some services, like Blogger and WordPress, offer an all-inclusive service comprising the platform, a unique web address (in the format myblog.wordpress.com), and hosting for free.

TypePad offers a similar all-encompassing online service with a monthly fee but more customization options.

Others are downloadable software that you have to install and host yourself. So although they offer the platform for free, you then need to find and pay for your own hosting and domain name and support it yourself. Others still might charge for a license for the platform, depending on how many blogs you have and whether they will have a commercial, personal, educational, or not-for-profit use, and then you need to arrange and pay for your own domain name and hosting on top.

## How Technical Are You?

This is a crucial factor to consider when choosing a blog platform. If you've never had any experience in creating a blog or website before and are not a technologically minded person, there are some blog platforms and setups that will be much more suited to your needs than if you know a few of the basics, or at least are willing to learn them.

The other option, of course, is to find someone who is a techie to help you out (either paid or as a friend).

One of the great things about blogging and most of the platforms is that there is a wonderful communal knowledge out there and many forums dedicated to helping people get the most out of their chosen platforms (see Figure 3-3).

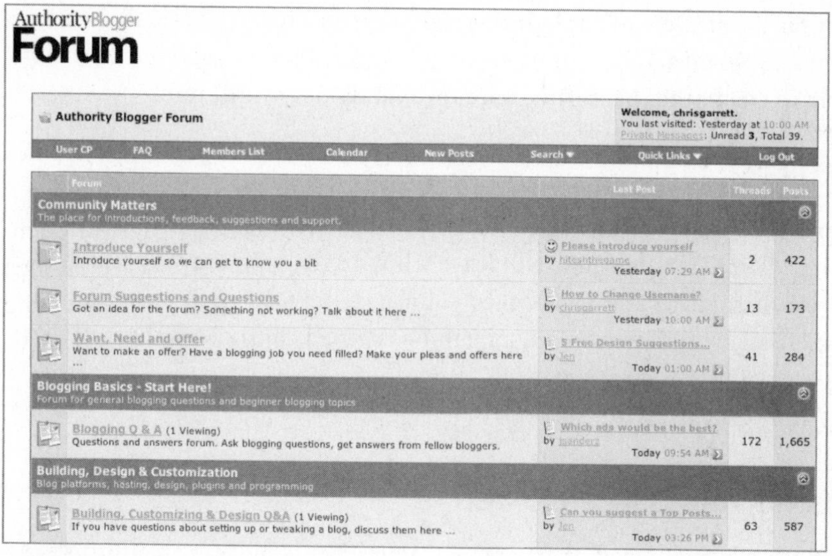

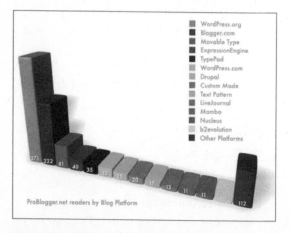

**Figure 3-3:** There are many helpful forums for bloggers.

## What Blog Platforms Are Others Using?

Though your blog is your own individual choice and should fit with your own style, it is worth looking around you to see what others, in particular people you know well, are using.

Over the past few years different platforms have come and gone, and you have to suspect this will continue to happen in the future. You can see in Figure 3-4 the results of a ProBlogger.net survey.

**Figure 3-4:** A 2006 ProBlogger.net survey.

By far the most popular platforms right now for pro bloggers are WordPress (both self-hosted and the online service), Blogger, TypePad, and Movable Type. We have tried other platforms, but now mainly use WordPress.

> **EXERCISE**
>
> Take a look at your favorite blogs; can you tell which platform they are using? Sometimes bloggers will leave a link to the software they use in the footer or sidebar, and sometimes you can tell by the URL (for example, something.wordpress.com or something.typepad.com). Does this software seem to offer you what you need?

## Hosted versus Self-Hosted

As previously mentioned, there are two main types of blogging platforms: software you install and host yourself, and online services that handle everything for you. These are often referred to as self-hosted blogs and hosted blogs.

### Hosted Blog Platforms

This is the type of blog that many bloggers start out with, simply because they are quick, easy, and can be free.

Probably the most popular of these systems with professional bloggers are TypePad, WordPress, and Blogger, with only TypePad having a monthly fee.

These systems are "hosted" blog platforms because they "host" your blog on their own domain. After what is usually a pretty easy setup process they will give you a web address (URL) that will usually be some combination of their own URL and the name of your blog, for example, `http://problogger.wordpress.com`.

Though this is what you get as a default, you are now often given the choice of paying a fee to use your own domain. This is something well worth considering if you are serious about blogging.

### Advantages of Hosted Blog Platforms

Using a hosted platform has many advantages. Some of the most immediate are listed here:

- **Cheap or free to run** — Most hosted options are free.
- **Quick and easy to set up** — Most of these types of blogs can be set up with a basic default template within minutes. The setup is usually just

a matter of filling in a few fields with your options and choosing a template design. They are ideal if you know nothing or very little about the technological side of blogging. You'll see more on this later.

- **Simple to run** — Once you're through the easy setup process, hosted blogs are usually pretty simple to run. You will obviously need to learn some basics, but these days most blog platforms come with very user-friendly features. Posting is as simple as filling in a few text boxes and clicking Publish.
- **Updated automatically** — If the blog platform changes, it will automatically upgrade for you. Instead of having to upload new software onto a server, these updates happen much more seamlessly.
- **Search engines and traffic** — One of the advantages of many hosted blog platforms is that they are hosted and linked from sites that already attract search engine attention and traffic. Some of this "rubs off" on your blog, giving it a little boost.

## Disadvantages of Hosted Blog Platforms

Although there are several benefits to having a hosted blog, there are always downsides:

- **Less configurable** — With an online service, the only configuration options you have available are those the service allows you. This may or may not be a problem for you, but in most cases you have fewer choices with a hosted service.
- **Default design limitations** — This can be true for standalone blogging systems, but many hosted blogs end up looking very similar to one another. This is because the default templates get used over and over again, and hosted platforms do not give you complete control over your look and feel.
- **Less ownership** — Another complaint I hear regularly from hosted-blog owners is that they are frustrated by not having ultimate control and ownership over their blog. Although they do own the content, the URL is not technically their own and they are somewhat at the mercy of their platform in terms of whether or not their blog is working.
- **Generic URL** — There are some very successful blogs on hosted platforms, but most bloggers believe that having your own URL is much more professional if you are using your blog in a professional way.

- **Upgrading or moving challenges** — One of the issues of starting out with a hosted platform is that, if there comes a day when you want to move, you have some work cut out for you in retaining your audience and traffic.
- **Non-commercial or lacking monetization options** — Most monetization options assume you have complete ownership and control of your blog site, and some hosted solutions forbid you to create a blog for commercial reasons.

## Who Might Use Hosted Blog Platforms?

If you just want a blog and don't care much about having your own unique domain and you are not too interested in tweaking your blog or getting all the latest and greatest features, hosted options are a completely valid choice.

In fact, it's worth keeping in mind that though some may scoff at hosted blog platforms and say that serious bloggers don't use them, there are some popular bloggers who have used them very successfully or got started that way. For example, three of my favorite blogs cut their teeth on hosted services: Scott Adams and Robert Scoble, started out with hosted blogs, and Seth Godin, still uses TypePad to this day (`http://sethgodin.typepad.com/`).

## Standalone Blog Platforms

The other type of blog platform is where you download, install, and host the software yourself.

This is what Darren and I do with all of our blogs these days. You will notice our blogs have their own domains, chrisg.com and problogger.net, and as I said before, we both use WordPress on our own server spaces.

Though we are fully in favor of people going the hosted route, you do get more control when you host your blog yourself. Of course, this is a double-edged sword!

## Benefits of Self-Hosted Blog Platforms

As mentioned before, both hosted and self-installed platforms have their own advantages and disadvantages. Here are the benefits of self-hosted blogs:

- **Full control** — Depending upon your ability with the technology and web design, standalone blogs generally are very adaptable. Although I am completely happy with the geekier aspects of blogs, I am not the best designer, so I tend to lean on others for aesthetics.

    There are designers out there who manage to create incredibly diverse and clever designs for blogs and provide for download both free and paid themes, so it should be possible to make your blog look fantastic.

- **Adaptability** — One of the things I enjoy about WordPress is the vast array of developers who are coming up with all manner of "plugins," which extend the ability of the basic WordPress installation. Many of the other standalone platforms have communities of developers producing similar add-ons.
- **Free platforms** — Although you end up paying for your domain name and hosting, systems like these are usually free to run. Some do have license fees, but most of the popular ones are free to use.
- **URL** — Having your own domain name is great for many reasons. For one, it's easier to remember; second, it's more professional; and third, it is more easily brandable.

## Disadvantages of Self-Hosted Blog Platforms

Although both Darren and I have our blogs set up this way, it could be the wrong choice for you for the following reasons:

- **Complicated setup** — Again, this depends upon your technical abilities, but when you move into standalone platforms the complexity of setup tends to increase. At the very least it involves arranging hosting and a domain name. There is a wealth of community support available, but for many it is still a daunting prospect.

  One way to simplify the process is to find a web host that provides "one-click installs" of popular packages. See how much easier this makes things later in this chapter.
- **Cost** — Although the blog platform itself might be free, you need to factor in the ongoing costs of having your own domain name (a yearly fee plus a one-off registration fee) and hosting fees (monthly or yearly). There are many great deals out on these, so it need not cost the world, but if your blog gets a lot of traffic, the costs can go up, and you might want to consider going onto a more professional, and therefore, more expensive plan.
- **Updates** — Most blog platforms go through changes and versions over time. Updating from one to another can be complicated if you don't know what you're doing.
- **Hosting issues** — I mentioned in the cons of the hosted platforms that you have "less control" over your blog and are at the whim of your platform's

hosting being up or down. Of course, this is also true for any hosting, because from time to time any hosting solution can have problems.

Whether you use a hosted solution or a standalone solution, it's important to back up and be aware that from time to time things do go wrong. Choose a reputable company to ensure maximum reliability.

### Who Would Use Standalone Blog Platforms?

Standalone blog platforms are ideal if you want a little more control or flexibility with your blogging. They can be configured to look and run very professionally and to be adapted into configurations that are limited only by your imagination.

If you host and control the blog yourself, you truly own it, with all that entails, including being able to sell your blog at some point for a profit.

Of course, just because you go with a standalone blog doesn't ensure you will have the perfect blog. In fact, if you don't have the ability to set up these blogs correctly (or know someone who can), standalone blogs can be messy and unprofessional.

This type of blog is what most people regard as the true professional option, and the majority of the world's top blogs are self-hosted.

## Hosted or Self-Hosted — Which to Choose?

To sum it all up, I generally advise people to go with self-hosted just because once it is set up, the hard part is over, and you have more potential to earn money directly with your blog.

If you want to develop a serious blog and have aspirations for it to be used on a professional sort of level (whether as a business or corporate blog, as a blog to build your own profile, or a blog to earn income from advertising) I'd always recommend you go in the direction of a standalone blog.

If you are not highly skilled in this area, it's worth spending a little time or money to get it set up right. You do not need to achieve perfection right away, and with a self-hosted option, the blog can grow with you.

Use a hosting company that features a one-click install of WordPress to make the initial setup far easier, and then you have to contend only with tweaking things to make them how you would like them.

If you want a blog only for fun, as an online diary for your friends and family, or you don't have the time, money, or patience to put into anything complex, a hosted option might work well for you.

They are instant (it'll take 5 to 10 minutes to set up), and although they might not have quite the same level of features and they restrict your income potential, the features they do have may well suit your needs.

**PROBLOGGER BLOG TIP: GET A FREE BLOG**

Regardless of which software you end up using eventually, it might be a good idea to play with some hosted services. It will help you get a clear idea in your head of which features and styles you like and any elements you find difficult to understand. Most online services are either completely free or have free trial periods that should give you plenty of time to work out how your chosen platform needs to work.

# Choosing a Domain Name

Having your own domain name is desirable for professional bloggers for several reasons. For starters, if you want to build credibility and a sense of professionalism around your blog, a domain can help. Similarly, a carefully selected domain name has the ability to enhance the branding and memorability of a product, service, business, or even person. Domain purchases give the added bonus of email addresses with the same domain (adding to both professionalism and branding) and can to an extent enhance your search-engine ranking.

## Factors to Consider When Choosing a Domain Name

Just as there are many factors to consider in choosing the name of your child, business, or pet, there are many implications of choosing names for a website.

What follows is a list of factors to keep in mind as you make the decision. Keep in mind that there are many theories about what is right and wrong in this area and that, despite all the rules that people have, there are some very successful sites that ignore them all!

Also worth remembering is that personal taste comes into decisions like this; what seems a good name to you will often mean different things to different people.

With those disclaimers in mind, take a look at a few areas to consider:

- **What are your goals and objectives?** We often come back to this point because where you are headed is such an important part of thinking about the long-term vision that you have for your blog. Might you want to eventually sell it?
- **What is the topic of the blog?** An obvious starting point, perhaps, but worth considering. Names can reflect the blog's topic or niche.
- **Why are you blogging?** For you, is blogging about having a hobby? Is it about building your profile/expertise? Is it about earning an income via ads? Is it to support an existing business ?
- **What style will it be?** Will you be blogging alone or will there be many authors? What length of posts will it have?
- **What tone and voice will it be written in?** Will it be conversational, newsy, rants, professional, or humorous?
- **Who is the intended audience?** Do you want to appeal to businesses, young people, cool people, Moms, locals, geeks ?
- **What is the source of traffic?** Domains can generate "type in" traffic; this is when people guess at or remember a domain name and type it in to the URL bar rather than search for it. This is why domains like business.com and sex.com sell for millions.

    On the other hand, domains can have an influence on search engines if the keywords are present in the name.
- **Branding** — Many discussions on domain name decisions talk about choosing between a domain name with keywords in it and domain names that are more brandable or generic. It's worth stating up front that it is possible to achieve both, but I would prioritize memorability and branding over keywords. One example that comes to mind is Engadget. com, which has become a memorable and well-branded name that also manages to incorporate the keyword "gadget."
- **Future directions** — Another factor to consider that is related to defining your goals and objectives is to consider what your blog might look like in the future. I've seen bloggers change their interests over time and be stuck with narrowly focused domains, or want to expand from having a blog to a larger community. Of course you can get a new domain, but it is less confusing and easier to market if you get it right from the word "go."

    Another "future factor" to consider is how many blogs you're thinking of starting on your domain. Take a look at About.com for an example of how it's possible to have one domain with many blogs running off it.

Lastly on the "future front" — don't pick a name that you suspect might date quickly. Picking a name that is time-specific in any way might find you searching for a new domain when it is no longer relevant at some future time.

- **Name length and spellings** —Opinions on what the ideal length of a domain name vary. Technically, you can have really long names and still be valid, but it is generally accepted that short ones are better.

  You want your audience to be able to quickly and easily say, spell, and remember your domain. The longer and harder it is to pronounce or spell, the less likely you will get good word of mouth.

- **Domain endings** — Along with the debates over domain name length come many different opinions over what is best to have at the end of your domain after the "dot." These letters (that is, .com, .net, .org, and so on) are technically called the Top Level Domains (TLDs) and are divided into two types. First there are country code TLDs, and second there are "generic" TLDs that signify different types of organizations (in theory, at least).

  There is a variety of approaches to selecting which TLD to go for, but unless you are targeting a specific country (for example, .fr for France) or have a particular legal or organizational structure to work within (for example, .edu for education), in general you ought to try for .com first, then try for the others, such as .org or .net.

- **Hyphens** — Another ongoing debate about domain names is over the value of hyphenated names. For example, a hyphenated version of Darren's blog might be Pro-Blogger.net. There are two main reasons that some people prefer hyphenated names:

  - **Availability** — One of the main reasons for going with hyphens is that all the good names are taken (or at least it can seem this way). Adding hyphens to names gives more options.

  - **SEO** — Hyphens are said by some to identify keywords to search engines more clearly. However, I have doubts as to how effective this is in the wider scheme of things.

  Of course, for every positive there is a negative, and the arguments against hyphens include the following:

  - **Memorability** — Adding hyphens can make it tricky for readers to remember your name.

  - **Difficult to communicate** — Have you ever tried to tell someone a domain name with a hyphen between each word? It can be quite an annoying process.

- **Increased margin for error** — The more characters in your domain name, the more chance of a mistaken keystroke.
- **Cheap and nasty factor** — There is a perception that hyphens are spammy. I personally don't mind a domain with one or maybe two hyphens maximum, but domains-that-have-lots-of-hyphens-turn-me-off. There are many bloggers who have been turned down when requesting links due to their spammy looking domains, so my advice is to avoid them.

- **Numbers** — Another option to consider when choosing a domain on a topic that is quite crowded is to include a number in it. Once again this increases your chances of finding a domain with your keyword in it but could add to confusion (do you spell out the number or not?).

- **Keeping it legal** — Think seriously about the legal implications of the words you use in your domain name, and avoid trademarked names especially. I know of a couple of instances where bloggers were forced into making changes months into new blogs because of legal threats.

- **The "blog" word** — One temptation for many bloggers is to use the word "blog" in the name and URL of their blog. I did this with the dslrblog.com domain. This has the advantage of opening up new options for domain names, but restricts the domain to being forever used as a blog and nothing else.

- **Secure multiple domains** — One piece of advice that many experienced webmasters recommend is making sure that you secure other similar domain names to the one you eventually choose. For example, if you choose a .com domain name it might be worth getting the .net and .org ones if you can, or perhaps even getting plurals or other logical, similar ones. This is not essential but might help you protect your niche in some circumstances.

- **Opinions of others** — Before you buy that domain you've been eyeing, it might be worthwhile to run it by one or two trusted friends (who won't run off and buy it for themselves). It's amazing how focused you can become on finding the right name and how that can cloud your judgment. It's also interesting to see how a name might sound to a person of a different culture. Words mean different things in different parts of the world, and it could help you avoid an embarrassing mistake or just a dorky blog name.

- **Previously used domain names** — It's worth checking to see if a domain has been previously registered. Spammers often buy domain names and then abandon them later once they've used them. This can leave these domains banned by Google, which might get you off to a pretty poor start. On the other hand, people abandon perfectly legitimate sites all the time, and an expired domain could be a bargain when you consider there might already be links pointing to it, or existing traffic.

## Registering a Domain

Registering a domain is much easier than choosing one! As you will see, when you order your hosting you can register a domain at the same time. The advantage to this is that your new blog is all set up with the new domain without you having to do any complicated technical stuff. You can order additional domains from your hosting company, too, for the same benefit, although you might find a better deal elsewhere with popular domain companies like GoDaddy.com or 123-reg.co.uk. Figure 3-5 shows one such service.

If you do register a domain with a company other than your hosting one, you will need to have the new domain pointed to your web host so you can take advantage of it. Check with your hosting company for details that you will need to supply to the domain company to do this, or get a technically minded friend to help you out.

**Figure 3-5:** Registering a domain independently of hosting.

EXERCISE

Brainstorm a list of potential blog names and associated domains, and then go through your list with a domain service such as GoDaddy.com to see how many are available. When you find a domain that is available, put a tick mark next to the entry. For any domains that are taken, go have a look to see what the owner has done with your chosen domain.

After you have a list of potential domains, rank them in order of preference and get feedback from friends and colleagues about which they prefer.

If you hit on a great domain, snap it up!

# Creating Your Blog

We have looked at the different options for building your blog and also some things to consider when selecting a domain name. I bet right now you just want to get on and create a blog already!

First, let's take a look at how easy it is to create a hosted blog at the WordPress .com online service.

## Four Steps to Setting up a Hosted Blog at WordPress.com

The easiest type of blog to set up is the hosted type, and by following these instructions, you will see just how easy it really is. If you can create a Hotmail or Gmail email account, you can build a blog!

1. Go to `http://wordpress.com/signup/` (shown in Figure 3-6).
2. Enter a username and a password choice. This username will be the name you use to log in but can also be the first part of your blog's web address — for example, username.wordpress.com. When you have filled out the form, click Next.
3. Next you will be asked to choose or confirm a blog domain, the title for your blog, your language, and if you want your blog to be discoverable by search engines (see Figure 3-7). If you are happy with your selections, click Signup.

**Figure 3-6:** www.wordpress.com

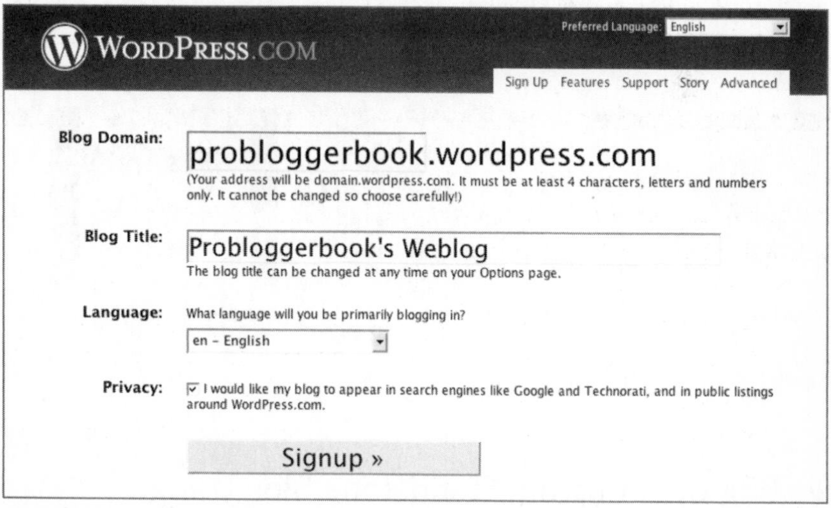

**Figure 3-7:** Enter your details.

4.  Now you need to choose a new look for your blog. Click Change Your
    Template. You will be able to choose from a variety of different themes
    (see Figure 3-8). Happy blogging!

**EXERCISE**

Register at the Problogger Book Member's Area and watch the WordPress .com video:

```
http://probloggerbook.com/?/register/bonus
```

(Make sure you type the address exactly as it is here.)

Set up a WordPress.com blog as demonstrated and use it to record a diary of your blogging progress and day-to-day thoughts. It will be good practice and will help you get into a "blogging mindset."

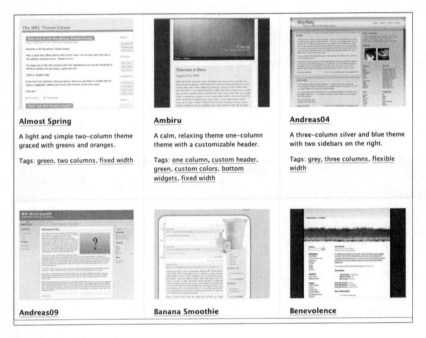

**Figure 3-8:** Select a theme.

# Setting Up a Custom Standalone Blog Using 1-Click-Install

The main advantage of a hosted blog is the ease of setup. As you have just seen, you can have a new blog in less than five minutes. For a pro blogger, though, a hosted blog will quickly show limitations and the pain of moving is far greater than setting up a custom blog in the first place. In this section I show you how easy it can be to set up a custom blog providing you use the right hosting company. What you are looking for is a hosting company that features a "1-click-install" of WordPress, or sometimes advertised as featuring the "Fantastico" system.

Before you sign up, you might already have a friend currently paying for hosting. Most of these services provide much more capacity than a single blogger ordinarily needs. Perhaps you can get a contact to host your blog for you? After you have generated some income, though, you would be wise to move to your own account.

### Creating Your Blog

To create your blog, follow these steps:

1. First you will need to sign up with a hosting service; for example, DreamHost (see Figure 3-9) and decide if you want to pay annually or monthly. Also at this point, you need to choose a domain name (see the earlier section for things to think about). This will be a proper domain in the form *something.com* so choose carefully. It's quite a long form, but it looks more complicated than it really is. Just take it slowly.

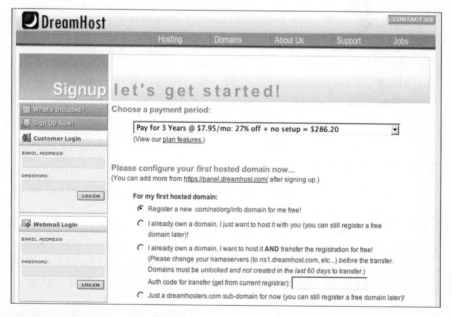

**Figure 3-9:** DreamHost's signup page.

2. You will be asked for your payment details. How long this process takes will depend on a number of factors, but eventually an email receipt will arrive, followed by an email confirming your new account. Other emails may arrive informing you of various other services that are ready to use.

3. At this point, you will have a hosting account and a domain registration. Your domain might not be visible for up to 24 to 48 hours, but that will not stop you from setting up your blog, and most people find it doesn't take that long.

4. When you log into your account you should see a list of options, normally down the left side. Under something like "Software" or "Goodies," you will find the "One-Click-Installs" option you are looking for (see Figure 3-10).

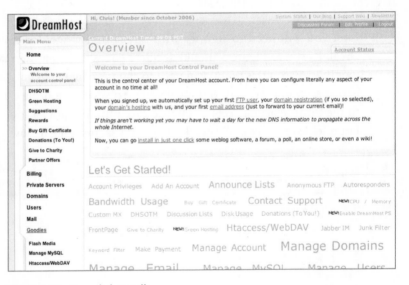

**Figure 3-10:** One-click installs.

5. Select "WordPress" (see Figure 3-11) and the domain you want to install it on.

It will also ask you for database and database host details; this is the database the system needs to create in order to store your blog posts. Don't worry about getting this wrong; just put in the name of your blog and **mysql** for the new hostname. Your screen will appear similar to Figure 3-12.

Within about 5 to 10 minutes, you will receive an email telling you your new blog has been set up. Simply go to the web address you requested.

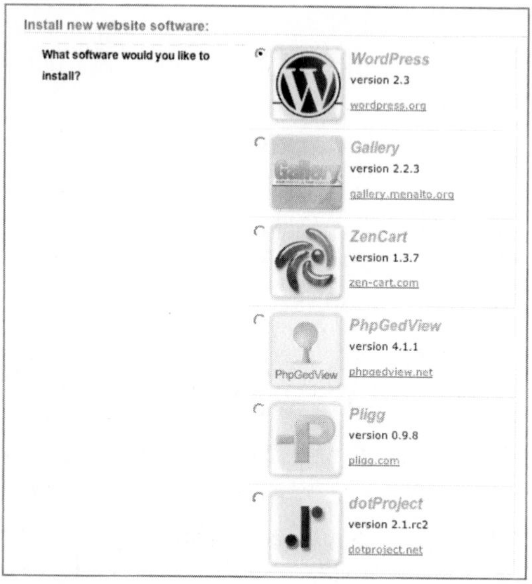

**Figure 3-11:**  Select WordPress.

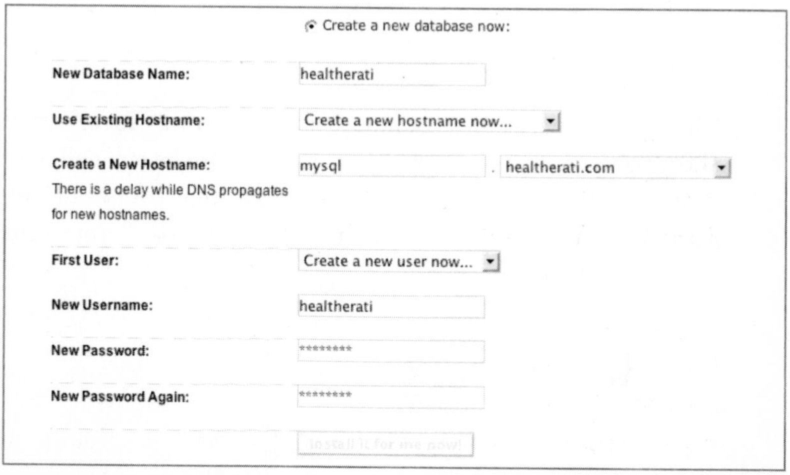

**Figure 3-12:**  The database details.

6. When you visit your domain, you will see a message from your new blog. Click the "install.php" link.

7. You will be asked for a blog title and your email address in a screen like that shown in Figure 3-13.

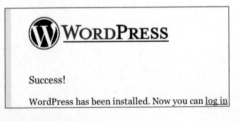

**Figure 3-13:** The blog details.

8. The next screen will let you know if the setup was successful and will show your temporary password, which will also be emailed to you. You only need this password to get in the first time; you can change it to something more memorable later. When successful, your screen will appear like Figure 3-14.

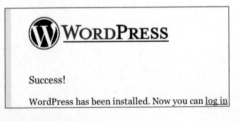

**Figure 3-14:** Success!

9. After logging in, you will be shown your dashboard, just like with the WordPress.com setup (see Figure 3-15).

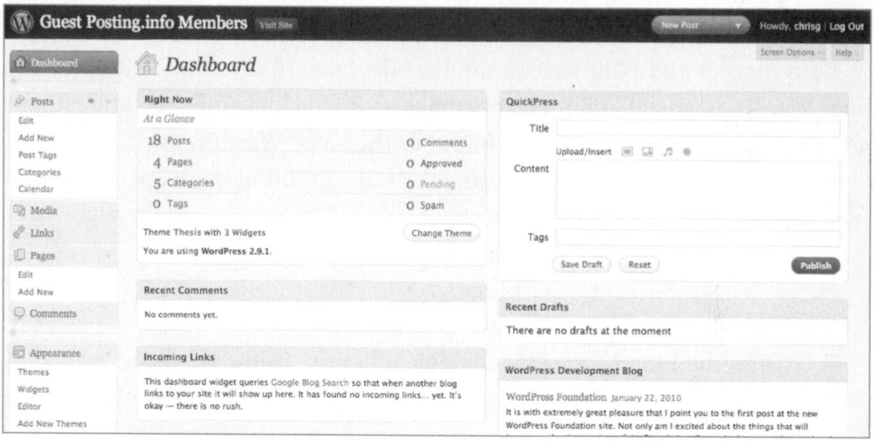

**Figure 3-15:** The WordPress dashboard.

Just like before you will be able to select a new theme. Go to "Presentation" and "Themes." Switch templates by clicking the one you like.

10. While your blog is now all set up you might want to take a look through the "Options" menu items in order to configure your blog exactly how you want it. Pay particular attention to "General," where you will want to set your tagline and date/time settings, and "Permalinks," where you can set WordPress to use a friendlier URL structure (for example, myblog.com/post-name/ rather than myblog.com/?p=123).

**EXERCISE**

If you have a hosting-company account already, check to see if they provide a one-click install of WordPress. Failing that, ask around for recommendations of hosting companies you might want to use. If your friends are no help you could always ask your favorite bloggers who they use; most would be happy to recommend their choice of hosting company.

If you have not already, go register at the Problogger Book Member's Area and watch the "One-Click Install" video:

```
http://probloggerbook.com/?/register/bonus
```

## Enhancing Your Blog

Once your blog is set up you will want to customize it to your specifications. WordPress makes this easier using themes and plugins.

Both themes and plugins are simply collections of files that you upload to your WordPress installation. Themes make your blog look different, and plugins add features or functionality not found in the basic WordPress.

The method of doing this is broadly the same for both; there are the built-in methods, and the "manual" methods.

To add a plugin using built-in tools, follow these steps

1. Log into your blog admin dashboard.
2. Go to the Plugins area by clicking "Plugins" in the left-hand menu.
3. Click the "Add New" button next to where it says "Manage Plugins" at the top of your screen.
4. Search for a plugin and click "install."
5. Alternatively, upload the file from your machine using the upload facility.

To upload a plugin "manually" using FTP, follow these steps:

1. Download a zip file containing your new theme or plugin.
2. Uncompress to get the actual files the zip file contains.
3. Upload to the appropriate directory of your blog using FTP.
4. Activate plugins using the "Plugins" menu item. Themes are selected exactly as they were using the bundled themes previously.

Plugins are uploaded to the `wp-content/plugins` directory of your blog; themes go into `wp-content/themes`.

You can find new themes in Appearance, Add New Themes, or at `wordpress.org/extend/themes/`, plus there is a list of plugins at `codex.wordpress.org/Plugins`.

One of the first plugins I always install is a contact form. This allows site visitors to get in touch via a simple form that will send an email to you on submission. In addition to making you easier to contact, it saves you from exposing your email address to the world. Unlike with a lot of plugins, there is an additional step required to implement it, which makes it a good example to demonstrate. Let's go through the process step-by-step now.

## Adding a Contact Form to Your Custom WordPress Blog

The following steps show you how to add a contact form to your self-hosted WordPress blog:

1. Search for the contact-form plugin using Plugins ⇨ Add New. The one I use is called "Enhanced Contact Form" and is by Joost Devalk.

2. Click "Install" to download and activate the plugin; then "Install Now", followed by "Activate Plugin."

4. You will need to configure the contact form in Options ⇨ Contact Form. Ordinarily, this would have activated the plugin and that would be all you would need to do. Your contact form, though, needs to live in a contact page, a page that you have to set up.

5. Go to Write ⇨ Write Page, and enter a title; something like "Contact Me" will do. You can enter any page content you like, but you will need to enter a special piece of HTML text for the form to show up. Enter the following exactly as shown:

   ```
   [wpcf]
   ```

6. On the right of the screen you will find "Post Slug," the page filename after publishing. Set this to "contact" — something short, meaningful, and memorable. Click "Publish."

7. Your page is created but nobody will be able to find it yet. Go to Presentation ⇨ Theme Editor and edit your "Header" or "Sidebar" depending on where you want to show the link.

8. Look for other page links, such as "About," that are already there and add your new one after it. In most cases links are kept in lists, so make sure you add your new link before the closing `</ul>` tag as here:

   ```
   <li><a href="/contact/">Contact</a></li>
   </ul>
   ```

9. Click "Update File," then take another look at your blog with the "View Site" link. All being well, your new contact form should show up in your navigation, ready to try!

# Blog Design Considerations

A lot of your blog's initial impact will be from your design. In the preceding section, we just chose a template off the shelf, but you will have much more success if you spend a little thought and effort on providing your blog with the perfect look.

Many people are put off by bad design before reading even a single word of content. A good design can really set off your content, make your blog appear more cared-for and professional, which can help you get those valuable subscribers.

Before selecting a design for a blog you need to decide some things:

- **What is your blog goal?** Are you aiming for AdSense profit, to sell products, fame? AdSense templates tend to free up more space for advertising, whereas if fame is your goal you will want a nice big sidebar area for your "About Me" box.
- **Who is your audience?** Funky? Straight-laced? Cutting-edge? If your target audience is the boardroom, you will need a more conventional design than if your audience is mostly made up of designers. This will influence your graphic and color choices.
- **What specific functions does the site need?** Certain templates have more abilities than others. Some are created to fulfill a certain purpose, such as templates for photo bloggers. Do you need header tabs? Randomized masthead images? Flexible block quotes? Here are some standard features you need to consider and allow space for:
  - Contact details
  - About or bio details/photo
  - Advertising
  - Archives by categories
  - Archives by date
  - Logo
  - Subscription buttons
  - Newsletter signup
  - Search feature
  - Blog roll
  - Recent posts list
  - Links to older key posts

# A Word on Color

As everybody knows, color affects mood. What do you want the mood of your blog to be? You will certainly get a different result with a pink blog than a grey one. Colors *mean* something as well as look nice. You know the classics:

- Red = passion, blood, anger
- Blue = conservative, business
- Green = nature, go
- Grey = formal, staid

Carefully consider what ambience you want to project and what possible meanings your color scheme should be associated with.

> **EXERCISE**
>
> Look around at blogs in your chosen niche. Find blogs outside your niche. What design styles do you like? Do any provide links to the theme or theme designer in their footers? Also browse online theme galleries and search Google for "WordPress theme." The more examples you expose yourself to, the more sure you'll be of your tastes and the better prepared you will be when it comes to building your blog the way you like it.

# Customizing a Blog Template

In most cases you will need to make your chosen template look unique. Your blog has to stand out and be unequivocally *yours*.

A nice template to use as a starting point is Cutline by Chris Pearson, as shown in Figure 3-16. You can get it from `http://cutline.tubetorial.com/`.

Although major template surgery is beyond the scope of this book (and my abilities!), the main two things people need to change are quite simple: the header image and colors.

## Changing the Header Image

Unlike most themes, Cutline has multiple header images depending on what sort of page you are on. Let's change that to just use one header image.

The images are stored under the Cutline images directory in `wp-content/themes`. They are 770-pixels-wide by 140-pixels-tall JPEG images. I am going to create a new header image of the same size in Photoshop.

After saving my image out, I upload it to the images directory. Just uploading my new image, though, will not make it appear; I need to alter the code that displays the header.

To do this I need to use the theme editor. This is in the Presentation menu ⇨ Themes ⇨ Theme Editor. The file to edit is `Header`. In Cutline the entire end of the `Header` file is all code to make different header images display.

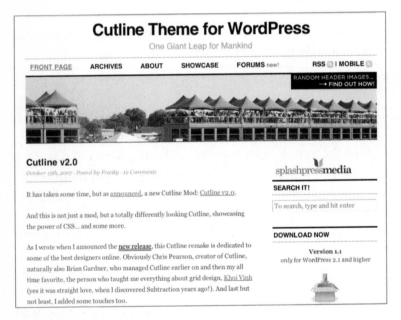

**Figure 3-16:** The Cutline theme.

Replace the code between:

```
<div id="header_img"> … </div>
```

with:

```
<img src="<?php bloginfo('template_url'); ?>/images/header.jpg"
width="770"
  height="140" alt="<?php bloginfo('name'); ?> header image 1"
title="<?php
  bloginfo('name'); ?>" />
```

This will make your new header appear all the time.

> **PROBLOGGER BLOG TIP: OUTSOURCING DESIGN**
>
> You might struggle to do your own design — this is fine; so do I! Though top-end design can be expensive, one of the great things about blogging is the community. It is possible to find excellent blog designers for far less than you might expect, especially when it comes to specific items such as header graphics. Ask around forums for recommendations, plus there are freelance communities like RentACoder (`www.rentacoder.com`), and do not overlook putting out a request on Craigslist (`www.craigslist.org`).

## Changing Colors

The other tweak you might want to make is to alter the color scheme somewhat. This is a little trickier because it means finding the correct part of the code to change and being careful with your edits so you do not break it.

In the Cutline theme you are provided a special `Custom.css` file to allow you to make your own changes without altering the original style sheet.

HTML colors use the hex numbering format with six digits representing the red, green, and blue values. I am going to change some of the elements to be red, which is represented as `#a00` (lots of red but no green or blue).

First I want to change the top menu link's "current" status from green to red:

```
.custom ul#nav li a.current, ul#nav li a.current:visited, ul#nav
li a.current:hover { color: #900; text-decoration: underline; }
```

This code looks a nightmare to anyone not used to it. We are only concerned with the "color" part, though, where I have changed the number to `#900`, a dark red.

Next I want to change the colors in the sidebar to match:

```
.custom li.widget h2, li.linkcat h2 { font-weight: bold; font-
size: 1.077em; text-transform: uppercase; letter-spacing:
normal; margin: 0 0 0.8em 0; padding: 0.4em 2px; border-top: 3px
solid #a00; background: #ddd url('images/hr_dot_black.gif') 0
100% repeat-x; }
```

Now the thick black lines are changed to red and the background of the headlines is a light grey (color `#ddd`).

## Further Customization

While you are editing the custom styles you might want to make a multi-functional masthead. Right now Cutline shows an image separate from your blog name; the following code makes them one and the same. You will need to remove the image we entered earlier in Header to make this work without showing two mastheads:

```
.custom #masthead { width: 770px; height: 100px; background:
#ddd
url('images/header.jpg') no-repeat; }
.custom #masthead h3 { margin: 0 0 0.75em 0; font-weight:
normal; font-size: 1.8em;
  text-transform: none; color: #a00; text-align: center; }
```

# Summary

We covered a lot of ground in a short chapter, so hopefully you were not overwhelmed!

The main point we hoped to make with this chapter is that setting up your blog need not be as difficult as it would first seem. Approach it with a feeling of fun and exploration, especially your first blog.

It is worth reiterating that the blog world is full of helpful people on forums and email lists. If any of the information we covered in this chapter confused you at all, the authors and the blogging community as a whole will surely be able to help you out.

# 4 Blog Writing

**M**uch has been written on what makes a blog successful, but all experts agree that central to all great blogs is one element: great content.

The cry, "Content is king," has echoed through the blogosphere for years; although I think the term ignores other aspects of what makes a blog successful, content is a key ingredient of a successful blog.

## What Is Good Content?

Defining good content is a subjective exercise (perhaps in a similar way to defining a good book or a good movie). Good content will vary from person to person depending upon their needs, the topic they are talking about, and perhaps even a person's ethics. Not only will bloggers themselves each have a different view on what good content is, but readers tend to also. I know that every time I ask for feedback about what I write about on ProBlogger, I get a real spectrum of responses.

Having said this, there are some things that can be said about good content, and in this chapter, we attempt to unpack some of them. At most points along the way there will be debate, but hopefully you will be able to mix and match the elements and identify what works for you.

So without any more introductory remarks, let's get into it with the first element of writing quality content.

## Usefulness and Uniqueness

Let me start our exploration of good content with a fairly obvious, but important, statement:

> *For a blog to be successful, your content needs to be useful*
> *and unique to your readers.*

It isn't rocket science, but two questions that bloggers need to continually ask themselves are, "Is my blog useful?" and, "How is it different from other blogs?"

Back in the days when I studied marketing, I remember sitting in lecture after lecture getting more and more frustrated as I listened to my lecturers drum into us the same thing time after time. Although they said it in different ways, the lesson that they communicated was largely the same in every instance and boiled down to this:

"Start with the customer — find out what they want, and give it to them."

This is a good lesson for bloggers also.

I would also recommend that you start with yourself as a blogger and blog out of your own passions, experiences, and knowledge, but it is essential that you be aware of your reader and that you create content that will add something to their lives.

Give them something useful and unique.

### What Is Useful Content?

Useful content to me is different from what it is to you, but could be any of the following:

- **Entertainment** — Increasingly, blogs are being used as entertainment. People are going to them for laughs, gossip, and fun conversation.
- **Education** — Some blog readers are primarily interested in learning something about a given topic.
- **Information** — Many successful blogs are built on the thirst that some have to be informed on an issue, product, or topic.
- **Debate** — Some blog readers want a place that they can have a good old-fashioned dialogue, debate, or even a fight over an issue.
- **News** — Many blog readers just want to be kept up to date with the latest news on a topic.
- **Community** — People have a desire to belong. Many successful blogs tap into this and are all about connecting people interested in exploring a topic. Quite often the topic is secondary to the actual relationship built on the blog.

Each blog has the potential to be useful in a different way, and it would probably be unwise to start a blog that tried to be all of these things at once (although many blogs do a variety of these things at once).

## Research Your Readership

The best advice that I could give on developing useful content is to research your readership (or potential readership). If you already have a blog, do this by surveying your readers (either formally or informally) or by asking for feedback.

I regularly ask my readers for questions, and much of what I write emerges directly from these queries.

Another quick tip for finding what questions your readers are asking is to check the referral statistics of your blog to see what words people are typing into search engines (SEs) to find your blog. A great little tool for this is Google Webmaster Tools, which tracks how people arrive at your blog and identifies questions being asked by your readers in search engines.

If you don't have a blog already, you'll need to work a little harder to research your potential readers. Survey friends, follow the comments sections of other blogs on your topic to see what readers are asking there, and look in forums and online discussion groups that cover your topics, where there is usually a lot of question asking going on.

As you do this you'll begin to put your finger on what people want and what you might be able to provide to meet these needs.

### EXERCISE

Who are your favorite blogs attracting? Why is that? Spend some time thinking about who you want to attract to your blog and the kind of work, lifestyle, and needs they have.

## Unique Content

Another factor to consider when thinking about good content is its uniqueness.

Technorati tells us that a blog is being created every second, and that there are ten of millions of blogs in existence today. This presents bloggers with the challenge of building a blog that stands out from the crowd.

I see blogs every day that provide "useful" content but that have no readers simply because people are finding that information in other places.

### Distinguish Yourself

New bloggers trying to break into a niche where others are already blogging should surf through the other blogs and websites in that niche and do some analysis on what sort of content those blogs and websites are producing.

In most niches, you'll find that sites are all presenting very similar information in pretty much the same voice, tone, and style. As a new blogger on the topic, you have a choice: You can either replicate what they are doing and try to do it better (difficult because they will already have loyal readers, and unless you're brilliant at it you're unlikely to convert these readers over to you), or you can distinguish yourself in some way from what others are doing.

This might mean focusing on a slightly different topic (perhaps a sub-niche), but could also mean writing in a distinct voice. (Take a look at Manolo's Shoe Blog for an example of a blogger who has grown a cult audience by writing about an odd combination of topics as an anonymous blogger writing in the third person.)

It might also mean writing in a different genre of posts. (That is, if everyone else is writing newsy posts, you might like to write more opinion-type posts.)

Bring together the elements of useful and unique in your content, and you will be one step closer to a successful blog.

# Writing Tips for Bloggers

Writing for the Web — and more particularly on blogs — is very different than writing in other mediums. In this section, we explore some practical tips for writing effectively as a blogger.

## Scannable Content

Web users are known for not staying on web pages long and for skimming through content rather than reading it word for word. This is even more the case when readers read through their RSS feeds. Rather than reading each word on a web page, web users scan pages for information, looking for keywords, phrases, and visual cues.

As a result, it is very important to learn how to write content that is scannable.

Here are a few tips and techniques you can use for working *with* your scanning readers instead of against them:

- **Lists** — This will be no surprise to ProBlogger readers — I'm pretty big on lists and my stats show me it's my posts with bulleted or numbered lists in them that get linked to and read *a lot* more than similar-length posts written in an essay style. You can see an example in Figure 4-1.

- **Formatting** — Use **bold**, CAPITALS, *italics*, <u>underlining</u>, and other formatting techniques to emphasize points. Don't go overboard, because you run the risk of frustrating your reader. Do be careful with underlining because it is also commonly used to indicate that text is a link. Also consider changing font size, color, and style to draw your readers' eyes to your main points.

- **Headings and subheadings** — Using headings midway through posts helps with post structure, but headings also are great for drawing your readers' eyes down the page and helping them find important points and the elements of your article that will most interest them.

- **Pictures** — Clever use of pictures in your posts can grab attention, emphasize points, and draw people down into your post. In a largely text-driven medium, images will give your post visual points of interest. I've tested how readers react to pictures in posts, and pictures are particularly effective at the top of posts to get people reading and worthwhile to break up the text in longer posts and to draw the eye to action items.

- **Borders/block quotes** — Boxes around quotes and key points can similarly get the attention of readers.

- **Space** — Don't feel you have to fill up every inch of your screen; rather, create spaces because they help readers not to feel overwhelmed and, again, tend to draw readers' eyes to what is inside such spaces.

- **Short paragraphs** — Web users tend to get lost in large blocks of text; break text into smaller bites, and you'll find people continue to read a post longer.

- **Don't bury your points** — Make your main points as clear as you can, and get your main point across in the first few sentences rather than bury it in your conclusion.

Work hard at producing content that can easily be scanned, and you'll find that your readers will stick with you, even through the longest of blog posts.

> **PROBLOGGER BLOG TIP: MAKE IT EASY**
>
> There are no points awarded for making your content complex, and your readers will not respect you any more if you use longer words. In fact, the reverse is probably true. Remember your reader might have poor eyesight, be distracted, or be in a rush. The easier you make your blog to read, the more readers you will attract.

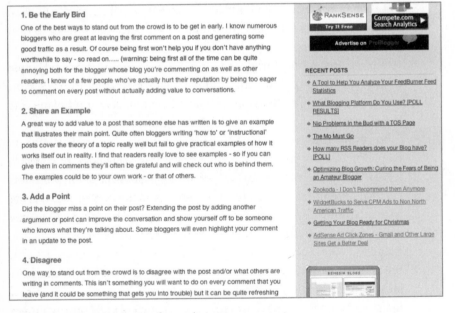

**Figure 4-1:** Lists make it easier for readers to scan content.

## Using Titles Effectively on Blogs

My mom drilled into me at a young age that first impressions are important. Outside of the design of your blog, perhaps the best way of creating that good first impression is through your post's title.

Well-written titles are important on many fronts, including the following:

- **Grabbing attention in search engines** — Go to Google and type in virtually any word you can think of, and you'll often find millions of results. The interesting thing is that for most search results in Google (and other search engines) there is very little for readers to go by in deciding which result to click on. There is a title, a short excerpt, and a URL. The most highlighted of these is the title, and I believe it is a key to getting search-engine-referral visitors.
- **Getting RSS readers' attention** — In a very similar way, titles have the ability to grab the attention of those following your blog via RSS feeds in news aggregators. News-aggregator readers tend to scan the titles of posts for things of interest rather than reading full text, stopping to read and visiting the posts that pique their interest. See Figure 4-2.
- **Getting attention in social bookmarking sites** — The same principle is true in social bookmarking sites like Digg.com and Delicious.com, which have the potential to send your site many thousands of visitors based almost solely upon the title of your post.
- **Loyal readers** — Good titles also impact the way your loyal readers interact with your blog. As I've already mentioned, web users scan pages, and one of the best ways to make them pause as they roll their eyes down your site is to capture their attention with a good title that intrigues them enough to slow down their frantic web surfing and actually read some of the content that you've poured time and energy into.
- **Search engine optimization** — Though there are many factors that contribute to how search engines rank a page of your blog, one of the most powerful onsite factors is the words that you use in the title of that page. By default most blogging platforms include your title in the title tags of your post's page and the URL structure of that page; both of these factors contribute to that page's search-engine ranking. Add to this that other bloggers often use your title to link to you (a very powerful thing), and your titles become a very important factor in ranking well and generating traffic in search engines.

**Figure 4-2:** Skimming a feed reader.

The title of a post is like an advertisement for it, and it can mean the difference between it being read and not, so learning to create great titles is a skill we highly recommend you learn.

## How to Use Titles Successfully

There are many strategies that successful bloggers use to draw attention to their posts with titles. There is no real right or wrong, and as with many aspects of blogging, what is a good title is subjective.

Ultimately the goal of your title is to get people to read the first line of your post. To do this, consider some of these techniques:

- **Keep it simple** — Most research that I've seen about titles argues that the most effective titles are short, simple, and easy to understand. Though breaking these rules can help grab attention (see the next item) they can also confuse, frustrate, and put a glazed look in the eyes of potential readers. Shorter titles are also good for search engines; keep it under 40 or so characters, and you'll ensure the whole title appears in search results in Google.

- **Grab attention** — Good titles set your posts apart from the clutter around them and draw readers into your post. Attention might be achieved using tactics of shock, big claims, controversy, or even confusion. Though these tactics do work at getting people in, it should also be said that they can do more damage than good if the rest of your post doesn't live up to the promises your title makes. By all means try to grab attention, just don't trick your readers into thinking you'll provide them with something you can't give them.

- **Meet a need** — An effective title draws people into reading more because they feel you've got something to say that they *need* to hear. Indexes like del.icio.us illustrate just how effective this is. Quite often the articles that get to the top of the list are "how to..." or "tutorial"-type articles that show readers how to solve a problem or need that they might have.

- **Describe** — Some readers are drawn into a post by a cryptic title that doesn't tell them much about what they'll be reading, but the majority of readers need to know something about what they'll find if they read further. Titles should describe what readers will get in the main post. They don't need to give away everything in the post, but being descriptive will definitely help.

- **Use keywords** — As I mentioned earlier, titles are a powerful part of SEO. If you want to maximize their power you need to consider using the keywords that you want your post to be found with in your title in some way. This, of course, is challenging when you are attempting to keep it simple and to also grab attention and intrigue, but it can be done. Words at the start of titles are thought to be more powerful than words at the end when it comes to SEO.

Take your time with the writing of post titles. Many bloggers pour a lot of effort into writing engaging and interesting posts, but then just slap any old title onto it without realizing that in doing so they might be ensuring that their post is never read.

Treat your title as a mini advertisement for your work. Take at least a few minutes before hitting Publish to not only make sure your post is in order, but that your title is going to do everything it can to maximize the chances that people will engage with what you have to say.

A great place to learn more about crafting your titles is CopyBlogger .com (Figure 4-3), which has a wealth of information on writing good copy for blogs.

**Figure 4-3:** www.copyblogger.com

### PROBLOGGER BLOG TIP: STEAL IDEAS!

Copywriters have a sneaky strategy for learning from the best writers. They steal ideas! No, this is not about plagiarism but using what they call a "swipe file." Whenever they come across a particularly effective headline, introduction, or turn of phrase, they take note of it for future inspiration.

Chris has posted a swipe file of 102 Headline Templates in the Problogger Book Member Download Area:

`http://probloggerbook.com/bonus/`

If you have not done so already, sign up here. Make sure you type the address exactly as shown:

`http://probloggerbook.com/?/register/bonus`

## Opening Lines Matter

The purpose of a post title is to get readers to read the first line of your post. However, to get people to read your full post, your opening lines are also crucial.

Readers will make a judgment as to whether your full post is worth reading based upon how it starts, and they will continue reading *if* you succeed in connecting with them on one of a number of levels.

Opening links should pique interest and curiosity, highlight a need that your reader has, show a benefit of reading on, and/or make some sort of promise to entertain, inform, teach, or offer something of value.

You don't need to do all of these things in the opening sentence of each post you write, but if you want your readers to reach the bottom of your posts and to be persuaded by what you write, you'll need to work hard early on at hooking them on some level.

## Post Length — How Long Should a Blog Post Be?

The optimal length of a blog post has been hotly debated by bloggers for years, and there are a number of factors to consider when thinking about it, such as the following:

- **Reader attention span** — It is pretty well documented that the typical web reader has a short attention span when it comes to reading content online. My own investigation into length of stay on blogs found that average blog readers stay 96 seconds. That's a minute and a half to communicate to your readers. As a result many webmasters purposely keep their content length down to a level that is readable in short grabs.
- **SEO** — There is a fairly strong opinion among those considered experts in search engine optimization that both extremely short and extremely long web pages are not ranked as highly as pages that are of a reasonable length. Of course, no one really knows how many words are ideal in the eyes of Google and its fellow search engines, but the general opinion seems to be that a page of at least 250 words is probably a reasonable length. Similarly, many advise keeping pages less than 1,000 words.
- **Quantity of posts** — One theory that goes around is that shorter posts allow you to write more posts and that more posts are better for generating readership with RSS and in search engines. Though I don't know

their strategy personally, some believe this is what sites like Engadget and Gizmodo do with the high quantity of short posts that make up the majority of their content.

- **Topic/genre** — The type of post that you're writing will often determine its length. For example, when writing a review of a product, you'll generally write a longer post than when you write a news-related post where you link to something someone else has written.
- **Comprehensive coverage of the topic** — Ultimately, this has to be the main criterion that bloggers go with. Write enough to comprehensively cover your topic and then stop. Long posts for the sake of them are not a wise move, but neither are short ones that don't cover the topic well.

My personal preference is to mix up my post length from post to post. I try to write one long post per day to give readers something meaty to chew on, but I also mix in short newsy posts most days.

## Post Frequency — How Often Should a Blogger Post?

One of the common pieces of advice that I see given to new bloggers is that they should write frequent posts on their blog.

This is good advice, but in my experience it's not quite as simple as that.

I think posting frequency is an issue that bloggers need to consider carefully on a number of fronts:

- **Writer burnout** — Every year, I do a 24-hour blogathon to raise money for a charity. Although I enjoy the process a lot, I find that it generally leaves me quite burned out — physically as well as in my ability to write. This is an extreme example, but it happens if your posting frequency is too high over a sustained period. The constant drive for high quality and relevant content is something that takes its toll on a blogger. Post too often and the quality of your writing could suffer.
- **Reader burnout** — Too many posts can also leave your readers burned out. I recently asked ProBlogger readers for the reasons that they unsubscribe to blogs, and "too many posts" was among the top reasons. I know from personal experience of reading blogs that if my news aggregator shows that there are more than 20 unread posts on a blog, I'm less likely to read each post in full and will unsubscribe from it if I can't keep up.

- **Reader participation** — Post too often, and you'll not give your readers enough space to have good conversations in the comments of your posts. Each time you post, you push recent articles further down the front page of your blog, making them less likely to be seen and responded to by readers. Also, there are only so many conversations that your readers can have at once. Post too many times per day and they'll feel overwhelmed and give up attempting to participate.

- **Search engine and RSS referrals** — One of the reasons to consider increasing your posting frequency is that the larger the quantities of quality content that you produce, the more open doors you have into your blog via both search engines and your RSS feed. Although you risk frustrating readers with high post levels, it generally leads to higher traffic.

- **Blog topic** — I'm a firm believer that there is no "one size fits all" approach to posting frequency on blogs. One of the main reasons for this is that different topics tend to lend themselves to different styles of blogging. For instance, a blog like Engadget has a very wide topic (consumer electronics/gadgets). This topic covers a lot of subcategories and to do it justice it needs to post a high number of posts (20 or more per day). Its readership knows this, and I suspect a lot of them want it, as they are attempting to keep up with a wider industry. Gadget lovers are also quite often information junkies who are usually tech-savvy and able to consume larger amounts of information. Other blogs with tighter topics would not be able to sustain such a large number of posts because there is only so much to write about on any given day.

- **Visitor type** — I've already touched on this a little (in saying gadget fans are often information junkies) but another way that your visitor type can impact posting frequency is the source of the visitor. For example, at ProBlogger.net I have a much higher readership that comes via RSS subscribers and bookmarks than on my digital-camera blog, which is largely visited by search-engine users and those coming from my email newsletter. As a result it is not as crucial that I keep my posting level down to a reasonable level on my photography blog, because it's not likely to impact many people. In fact, having more posts can be helpful because it means there are more landing points for SE traffic.

- **Post length** — Another observation that many people make about some of the most highly visited blogs is that while they post a lot more frequently than other blogs, their post length is shorter, making the high number of daily posts less annoying.

- **Momentum** — Posting too much can burn out your readers, but not posting enough can be just as frustrating. If readers subscribe to your RSS feed or, newsletter, or bookmark you, they are actively inviting you to communicate with them. When you don't, it can be quite annoying. On weekdays, I have a once-per-day blogging minimum for my own blogs. Other bloggers establish a weekly rhythm and find that it works for them, but I like to produce something daily, which builds an anticipation and momentum with readers that helps to grow the blog.

- **Rhythm and consistency** — When it comes to post frequency, it is important to find your blogging rhythm and stick to it. Though readers don't want you to be monotonous in terms of *what* you write, I've found they do quite often want it in terms of *how* you write — and more specifically, in *how often* you write. People want to know what to expect; they buy into things that they know fit in with their own rhythm of life, so if you start out writing daily but then increase the frequency to hourly, you'll probably find people reacting against it (and the same goes the other way around).

Posting frequency will vary from blog to blog, and you should experiment with different ways of doing it as your blog develops. If you are just starting out, attempt to post to your blog four or five times a week while you're finding your feet; over time you'll find a rhythm develops that suits you and your readers.

**EXERCISE**

Take a moment to think as a reader. How often do you like your most visited blogs to update? Do you visit each blog every day? Have you ever found a blog you liked that posted too often? Not often enough?

# Keep Posts Granular

One topic per post — we've already spoken in this book about choosing a niche topic for your blog, but another strategy of many successful blogs is that in addition to having an overarching niche topic, they tend to have each post focus upon a more tightly targeted topic.

On some levels this is a fairly natural and logical thing that most bloggers do, but occasionally I come across a blog post that seems to want to answer every question known to humankind in a single post. The result can be a long, unfocused, rambling post that doesn't really go anywhere.

Instead of feeling you need to stuff everything into one post, a strategy that often works better is to be more granular in the way you post (that is, break it down into grains).

In effect you end up with a blog that can be shown visually like Figure 4-4.

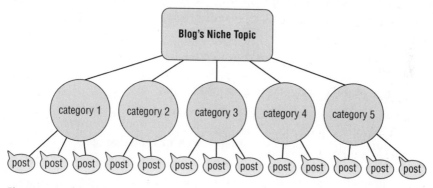

**Figure 4-4:** Blog granularity.

These categories are important for many reasons, including these:

- **Niche topic** — Your overall blog has a niche topic or focus — something we talked about earlier.
- **Categories** — Within the niche, you have categories that break the overall topic into smaller parts. (For example, at ProBlogger.net, I have a category for blog design, writing content, and blog tools.)
- **Readability** — Some of your readers will not be interested in the whole niche that you are writing about, but instead will want to look only at part of it (one or two of your categories). Category pages become, in effect, like a mini blog within your whole blog, which can help readers find and follow the elements of the topic they are interested in.
- **SEO** — Search engines like information that is clustered together and linked to other information like it. This is one of the reasons that niche blogs work well in search engines. Categories help this further, with

category pages often ranking well in SEs. They also help the SE bots that come to scan your site to get around easily (important for getting your whole site indexed).

- **Posts** — Your categories will then be broken down even further into posts.

Each post will not cover the whole category (unless your categories are very small) but will cover an element of it. Tightly focusing your posts on different elements of your category will help you round out your whole niche topic.

This structure is quite similar to that of a book, which has an overall topic, chapters, and then sections.

## Benefits of Granular Posts

Writing in a granular style has numerous benefits:

- **Ease of use** — We've already talked in this book a number of times about how people don't stay long on websites and that blog readers have short attention spans. Granular posts help with this. They are shorter and punchy and go directly to the point.

- **SEO** — Pages with single topics make it easy for search engines to work out what your post is about. This helps them to rank you accurately for the topic you're writing about.

- **Contextual ad relevancy** — Similarly, having only one topic helps contextual ad systems like AdSense determine what you're writing about and serve relevant ads for that topic.

- **Ease of writing** — This is more of a personal reflection than anything, but I find it easier to concentrate on one topic at a time. I'm much more productive in this way.

- **Granular does not equal short** — One of the criticisms I've seen of the idea of granular posting is that some people like longer posts. I would argue that granular posts need not be short at all. Some of my most popular posts are tightly focused upon a single topic, but are quite long.

- **Utilizing a series of posts** — One option for those bloggers who find it difficult to write in a granular style is to break their longer, general posts down into a series of posts. In fact, I quite often start out writing a post on a topic and find that it'd be much too long and diverse to be read all at once. We cover how to write a series of granular posts later in this chapter.

**PROBLOGGER BLOG TIP: KEEP IT SIMPLE**

Granularity is just one way that keeping your blog simple can benefit you and your reader. So many bloggers try to overcomplicate things when simple and easy can be just as effective, and it keeps your stress level down!

# 20 Types of Blog Posts

One of the traps that I see some bloggers fall into is that their blogs often become quite one-dimensional in terms of the type of posts they write.

Mixing up the types of post that you write can add variety and character to your blog, which will help to keep readers over the long haul.

There are many types of posts that you might like to use; here are 20 to start experimenting with:

- **Instructional** — Instructional posts tell people how to do something. I find that posts that contain tips or that are tutorials generally are the ones that are among my most popular. One of the main things that people search the Web for is to find help in overcoming a problem. Position yourself to answer these problems, and you can build a nice source of traffic over the long term.
- **Informational** — This is one of the more common blog post types, where a blogger simply gives information on a topic. It could be a definition post or a longer explanation of some aspect of the niche that you're writing on. This is the crux of successful sites like Wikipedia.
- **Reviews** — Another highly searched-for term on the Web is "review." Every time I'm considering buying a new product I head to Google and search for a review on it first. I know that I'm not alone. Reviews come in all shapes and sizes and on virtually every product or service you can think of. Give your fair and insightful opinion and ask readers for their opinion; reviews can be highly powerful posts that have a great longevity.
- **Lists** — One of the easiest ways to write a post is to make a list. Posts with content like, "The Top Ten ways to...," "7 Reasons why...," "5 Favorite...," or "53 mistakes that bloggers make when..." are not only easy to write, but are usually very popular with readers and can be successful at getting links from other bloggers.

- **Interviews** — Sometimes when you've run out of insightful things to say it might be a good idea to let someone else do the talking in an interview. This is a great way not only to give your readers a relevant expert's opinion, but to perhaps even learn something about the topic you're writing. One tip if you're approaching people for an interview on your blog is don't overwhelm them with questions. One or two good questions are more likely to get you a response than a long list of poorly thought-out ones.

- **Case studies** — Another popular type of post is the case study, where you walk readers through an example of something that you're writing about. These are useful posts for readers because they are real-life situations and often have practical tips associated with them.

- **Profiles** — Profile posts are similar to case studies but focus in on a particular person. Pick an interesting personality in your niche and do a little research on them to present to your readers. Point out how they've reached the position they are in and write about the characteristics that they have that others in your niche might like to develop to be successful.

- **Link posts** — The "link post" is a favorite form of blogging for many bloggers and is simply a matter of finding a quality post on another site or blog and linking up to it. You would usually also include an explanation of why you're linking up, a comment of your own take on the topic, and/or a quote from the post. Adding your own comments makes these posts more original and useful to your readers. The more original content the better, but don't be afraid to bounce off others in this way. These link posts are powerful because they not only give your readers something good to read, but they can get you noticed and help you build relationships with other bloggers.

- **"Problem" posts** — Another term that is often searched for in Google in conjunction with product names is the word "problem" or "problems" — that is, where people are searching for help on a problem that they might have with something that they own or are trying to do. Problem posts are similar to review posts, but focus more upon the negatives of a product or service. Don't write these pieces just for the sake of them, but if you find a genuine problem with something, a problem post can work for you.

- **Comparison posts** — Life is full of situations that require you to make decisions between two or more options. Write a post contrasting two products, services, or approaches that outlines the positives and negatives of each choice. In a sense these are review posts but are a little wider in focus. I find that these posts do very well on some of my product blogs where people actually search for "X Product comparison to Y Product" or "X vs. Y" in search engines.

- **Rants** — Get passionate, stir yourself up, say what's on your mind, and tell it like it is. Rants are great for starting discussion and causing a little controversy; they can also be quite fun if you do them in the right spirit. Just be aware when you write passionately about a controversial topic that others are likely to comment in a similar way. Rant posts lead to flaming in comment threads and to people saying things in the heat of the moment that they later regret, and that can impact their reputation. Proceed with caution.

- **Inspirational** — On the flip side of the angry rant (and not all rants have to be angry) are inspirational and motivational posts. Tell a story of success or paint a picture of "what could be." People like to hear good-news stories in their niche because it motivates them to persist with what they are doing. Find examples of success in your own experience or that of others and spread the word.

- **Research** — In the early days of ProBlogger, I wrote quite a few research-oriented posts where I'd carry out surveys or gather statistics on different aspects of blogging. Research posts can take a lot of time, but they can also be well worth it if you come up with interesting conclusions. Present your findings with a nice chart and with useful statistics, and you'll often find other bloggers in your niche will link up to you.

- **Collation posts** — These are a strange combination of research and link posts. In them, you pick a topic that you think your readers will find helpful and then research what others have said about it. Once you've found their opinion, you bring together everyone's ideas (often with short quotes) and tie them together with a few of your own comments to draw out the common themes that you see. These posts are often quite interesting to readers, but can help you build relationships with others blogs who you quote and link up to.

- **Prediction and review posts** — We see a lot of these at the end and start of the year when people do their "year in review" posts and look at the year ahead and predict what developments might happen in their niche in the coming months. Prediction posts will often cause interesting debate.

- **Critique posts** — Numerous bloggers have made a name for themselves by writing strong critiques of other people, products, or companies. Though sometimes these border on being "attack posts" and have rant-like qualities, a good constructive critique can be an effective way of making an impression upon others. People like to hear opinions, and although they might not always agree with them, if they are insightful, constructive, and respectfully written posts, they can lead to you growing your reputation in a niche.

- **Debate** — I used to love a good debate in high school; there was something that I quite enjoyed about preparing a case either for or against something. Debates do well on blogs and can be done in an organized fashion between two people, between a blogger and "all comers," or even between a blogger and… themselves. (Try it; argue both for and against a topic in one post. You can end up with a pretty balanced post.) Probably the easiest way to do this is simply to ask your readers a question with two or more alternatives and see what they've got to say. Be willing to share your own opinion to get things going.

- **Hypothetical posts** — "What if" or hypothetical posts can be quite fun. Pick something that could happen down the track in your industry and begin to unpack what the implications of it would be. "What if Google and Yahoo! merged?" "What if Canon released an update to xyz camera?" These posts can actually position you well in search engines if the hypothetical situation actually happens.

- **Satirical posts** — Well-written satire, parody, or humor can be incredibly powerful and is brilliant for generating links for your blog. Keep in mind that sometimes these types of posts will be misinterpreted and people will react strongly.

- **Memes and projects** — A meme is an idea that spreads, an "idea virus" as Seth Godin would describe it. In blogging this can be seen as an article or topic that gets copied from one blog to another, usually with a link back to the originator. Write a post that somehow involves your readers and gets them to replicate it in someway. Start a poll, an award, a competition, or ask your readers to submit a post/link or run a survey or quiz. These types of posts add an element of interactivity to your blog and sometimes can go viral through the blogosphere.

This is not an exhaustive list, but rather just some of the types of posts that you might like to throw into your blog's mix.

Not every one will be suitable for all blogs or bloggers, but using more than one format can definitely add a little spice and color to a blog.

**EXERCISE**

Next time you read a blog post, try to identify which category from our list the article comes under. How has the author added her own unique spin? Are there any tips you can take away?

# 10 Steps to Writing a Successful Series on Your Blog

One effective way of building momentum on a blog is to write a series of posts that build upon one another and explore a topic over a number of days.

Writing a series will give readers a reason to come back to your blog over a period of time, but it will also enable you as a blogger to create multiple bite-sized posts on a larger topic, making the writing process easier and yet still comprehensively covering the topic.

Though writing a series can seem like an overwhelming task at first, it needn't be. Here's the workflow that I use to create one:

1. **Identify a topic.** This is, of course, key when it comes to developing a successful series (as it is with single posts). As I reflect upon most of the series of posts I've written at ProBlogger.net over the past year, it's interesting to see that in virtually every case the series has started in my mind as a single post that grew into something bigger. The key is to make sure you choose a topic that is large enough to warrant multiple posts (you don't want to write a series just for the sake of it), but manageable enough not to overwhelm you. Some topics are so large that they could almost be a blog in and of themselves.

2. **Write a list.** When I make the decision that a topic is big enough for a series, I start with a brainstorming session and compile a list of the main points that I want to make. These lists generally start out as bullet-point lists of keywords and phrases written up either in a text document or a notebook. Once I've got a list of main points I then go back and add a few descriptive sentences to each one to describe what I want to say. It's

amazing how many of these sentences make it into eventual posts. I find that once I'm on a roll a lot of it just flows and I can end up with a list of 10 or so ideas pretty quickly. The list is rarely the final list of points that I end up publishing (some don't make it and others are added), but it does form the basis for my series, with each point usually ending up as a post of its own; remember we're aiming for granular posts.

3. **Set targets.** At this point I set myself some goals for the series and establish boundaries for it. Looking at the list, I can generally tell how many posts I'll need to complete it, which in turn helps me decide for how long it will run. I usually try to run them for a one-week period (starting on a Monday and ending on a Friday), but have been known to run them over longer and shorter time frames.

4. **Set up draft posts.** With these details settled, I then take the list I've created and whatever I've written for each post so far (often just a few keywords and a sentence or two) and copy and paste them into some draft posts on my blog. I give each one a draft title (often changed later) and just leave them each there as drafts for me to work on in the coming days.

5. **Pick a series title.** The name that you give your series is a very important factor in its success and I would recommend that it be something you give serious consideration to. The title of your series is an advertisement to readers and will draw them into it. Readers decide on first impressions whether they will read a post, and they do the same with a series. If you don't capture their imagination with the first post of your series, they are unlikely to read those that follow. The way to pick the title for a series is pretty similar to the process of choosing one for individual posts, and is often a combination of something that is catchy and something with some good keywords in it (for SEO purposes).

6. **Announce the series.** Up to this point all my work is in private, but I put the pressure on myself now by announcing the series with an introductory post. This serves a number of purposes, including letting your readers know what to expect. (It creates some anticipation.) It also makes me accountable for finishing what I've started. There's nothing like telling your readers that you'll be writing X number of posts on a topic to keep you motivated and accountable for the task. Encourage readers to subscribe to your feed at this point in order to follow your post.

7. **Write an introduction to the series.** The announcement post will also include an introduction to the topic. It includes where you'll be headed

over the coming days. (You may want to name the actual topics you'll be covering.) The other thing that this post will do is to help highlight the "need" that the series will help to address. I'm a firm believer that the most successful series of posts that I've written have been popular because they meet some sort of need that people have, so help readers to see why tuning into your blog in the coming days will be important.

8. **Write a post per day.** My workflow is to write posts in a series on a daily basis. Some bloggers prefer to write them all in advance, but I like to keep them fresh and to not only build upon what I've written the previous day, but what readers have written in the comments on those posts. I also find that writing a lot of posts all at once can be a little too overwhelming; breaking it down into bite-sized pieces is much more manageable for me.

9. **Interlink your posts.** I see a lot of bloggers attempting to write blog posts as a series but not joining their posts with links. Though your current regular readers will be able to follow your post by logging on each day or reading it in RSS, future readers of your blog might not have as much luck. They often come in via a search engine to a middle post in the series and if you haven't linked to the rest, they will have to go searching for it. You can interlink your posts easily enough by linking to them all on the introductory post to your series and by linking back to that introduction at the beginning and end of each post (telling readers that they'll find the full series there). Alternatively, you can link to the preceding and next post in the series in each post, making it like a chain from one to the next.

10. **Finish your series well.** Though it might sound obvious to finish your series, I think it's important to do this well. If you don't have a definite end, a series can fizzle toward the end and some readers will feel that they've been left hanging. Summarize the series and the main points and invite readers to add their own points, sharing what they think you might have missed.

Learning the art of creating a good series is something that can bring a lot of life to your blog. I try to do one at least once a month, and I find that readers generally respond to them very well. They work particularly well if they are teaching-oriented, practical, and connected with a real need that your readers have.

At ProBlogger my most effective series have included the following:

- Blogging for Beginners
- 31 Days to Building a Better Blog
- Battling Bloggers Block
- 7 Days to Rediscovering Your Blogging Groove

In each case the series was very practical and connected to a need felt by my target audience—bloggers.

**EXERCISE**

Brainstorm some potential series topics for your blog. Which subject areas can you write consistently about over a number of days? Now take the most promising ideas and sketch out the contents in bullet points. Before embarking on any series it is a good idea to have a roadmap of the key points you will cover.

# Building an Interactive Blog by Encouraging Comments

The beauty of blogging is that it is conversational in nature. You as a blogger start the conversation and others respond in comments on your blog or in posts on their own. Work with this and write in a way that invites others to participate, and you'll grow a more dynamic blog. Here are a few quick tips on getting more comments for your blog:

- **Invite comments** — It sounds too easy to be true, but people are more likely to comment when you ask them to. Give a call to action to comment, and people will.
- **Ask questions** — Including specific questions in posts definitely helps get higher numbers of comments. This is particularly the case when the question is asked in the title of the post.
- **Be open-ended** — If you say everything there is to say on a topic, you're less likely to get others adding their opinions because you'll have covered what they might have added.

- **Interact with comments left** — If you're not willing to use your own comments section, why would your readers? If someone leaves a comment, interact with them. Doing so shows your readers that their comments are valued, it creates a culture of interactivity, and it gives the impression to other readers that your comments section is an active place that you as the blogger value.

- **Be humble** — I find that readers respond very well to posts that show your own weaknesses, failings, and the gaps in your own knowledge rather than those posts where you come across as knowing everything there is to know on a topic.

- **Be controversial** — There's nothing like controversy to get people commenting on your blog. Of course, with controversy comes risk and the potential for being attacked, so use with caution.

- **Reward comments** — Reward good comments by highlighting them on your blog. Drawing attention to your readers who use comments well affirms them, but also draws attention of other readers to good use of your comments section.

- **Establish boundaries** — Occasionally the comments section on a blog can descend into something of a squabble. Establish boundaries up front on what is and isn't acceptable in comments. You even might like to post this as a comment policy. Ultimately it is your blog and the rules you set are up to you to decide. Having boundaries will help your readers to know what is and isn't acceptable and can help you in your comment moderating.

- **Shape your blog's culture** — I am increasingly aware that bloggers set the tone for their blog's "culture." It is important to note that readers will usually take your lead when it comes to the tone they use in comments. If you write posts in an angry and personal attacking style, expect to see this reflected in your comments section. If you model a more inclusive and friendly style, the majority of your readers will follow your lead in this also.

Don't get too down if people don't comment on your blog with great frequency. Even the most popular blogs tend to attract only about a one percent commenting rate on them! Persist with the preceding techniques, and you'll build a blog that not only grows in traffic, but one that truly engages with people and develops a culture of community.

**EXERCISE**

Make a note of blogs you frequent that manage to create a vibrant community feel and those that barely manage to generate any comments at all. Can you see anything in common between them? Which ways do the bloggers draw you in?

## Summary

There is no doubt about it: Blogs are all about content. Without great content you will not attract an audience and you will never achieve your blogging goals.

The topic you write about is only the start; you need great headlines, formatting, an appropriate type of post for the subject, and to bring your readers into the community you are building and keep them engaged. Hopefully after reading this chapter, you have ideas about how to make this happen in your blog.

# 5

# Blog Income and Earning Strategies

There is no single right way or wrong way to earn money from blogging. If you compare the approach Darren uses with the one I use, you will see quite a distinct difference. Cast your net wider, and you will be hard-pressed to find two bloggers who make money identically. This is a good thing!

The opportunity is there for any blogger to make some money, and to do it in a style that works for them. Each blog and every blogger is different. The opportunities vary depending on your own abilities, the opportunities presented by the niche, and even your own specific audience.

Though not every blogger will achieve the huge paydays that some bloggers achieve, there are many bloggers doing quite nicely through the tactics I describe in this chapter.

## Time to Make Money?

The first decision you have to make is obviously whether you even want to try making money. There are many bloggers who swear off any sort of commercialization of blogs, and then there are others who try and do not like it.

I'm going to assume you do want to make money off your blog. The two questions then become:

- When?
  and:
- How?

When to monetize is a question with no correct answer. Ask around and you will get many forthright answers, none of which helps very much.

There are two dominant camps of opinion on this question, both of which have their own merits:

- **Run ads from day one** — The idea here is if you're thinking of running ads eventually, you might as well integrate them from the start. The reasons you might want to do this include the following:
  - **Reader expectations** — Starting a blog with no ads and then adding them later means running the risk of disillusioning readers whose expectations are that the blog is and always will be "ad free." Some readers feel very strongly about this and changing the rules mid-stream can cause problems. Start with ads from the beginning, and you set the expectations from the start and don't cause any upset later.
  - **Consistent design** — Running ads from the beginning of your blog keeps everything consistent, which is good from a reader-comfort and branding point of view, and also means that you don't need the hassle or expense of a redesign later on to accommodate ads.
  - **Earnings** — Darren's blogs were ad-free for months until he implemented AdSense; he regretted his delay later, after seeing what he could have earned. Put ads on your blog from the start, and you'll begin to see some money from the early days. Of course, it might not amount to a lot, but you could be pleasantly surprised.
  - **Ad-optimization experience** — It takes time to learn how to tweak ads. Most of us learn best through personal experience rather than by just reading about it. The great thing about starting early with advertising is that you can experiment and try different techniques without too many people seeing the mistakes that you make along the way. This means that by the time the traffic does start to come in, you can have your ads optimized to take advantage of it.
- **Establish readerships and then run ads** — Rather than put ads in right from the start, there is an equally valid argument for keeping them off until you have built an audience. This argument is basically that if you put ads on your blog too soon, you could potentially turn people off your blog because it will look too commercial or like too much of a money grab.

The thought is that you can gradually add advertisements later once you've established some trust, gathered a sizeable readership, and you have built up lots of good-quality links that serve to enhance your search-engine visibility.

As mentioned earlier, Darren launched this way initially and his most recent blog, Digital Photography School (`http://digital-photography-school.com/blog/`; see Figure 5-1), was only lightly monetized at launch, which I am sure helped him gather his huge audience. I have personally used both approaches, as I will explain later.

Ultimately the decision to add advertising to a blog is a personal one, and neither approach will work for everyone.

**Figure 5-1:** Darren launched his most-recent blog with little monetization.

## Factors to Consider

How do you know whether to hold off with the ads or put them in place right now? When deciding which approach to use, consider the following:

- **How commercial is your niche?** I used to own a photography blog all about a type of camera called a DSLR, hence I named it DSLRBlog. People who follow the topic tend to be heavily into equipment and therefore ads are not just tolerated, they are practically encouraged, so right from the start I would feature advertisements and affiliate links in reviews. Other niches will be very anti-commercialism and therefore a lighter touch will be needed.

- **Is it worth it?** You might find the only advertising you can show from the start is poorly paying, untargeted AdSense. If you are getting only one or two clicks a day at some tiny amount per click, you might find there is not much point in adding advertising until you have an audience and the content to allow you to earn from it. In most cases you can use your advertising spots to show affiliate ads or advertising for friends to make your blog more attractive to potential paid advertisers, but it is worth considering as part of your decision.
- **Will ads detract?** If your primary monetization strategy is to use indirect methods or sell your own product, you might want to concentrate on using your blog real estate for those channels. Also, you have to consider how tacky the advertisements tend to be in your niche. People are much more likely to overlook ugly advertising in an established blog than a new one. You don't want to damage any fledgling trust you are building with off-putting ads.

Again, choosing whether to show ads is a personal decision that's driven as much by financial pressures as personal taste. Luckily there is no right or wrong answer, and the presence of ads is no longer held in as much suspicion as years ago.

## Monetizing Directly with Advertising

Advertising is by far the most popular monetization method that bloggers use. After deciding to show ads, your next decision is which type.

The most popular advertising system with bloggers is Google's AdSense, but there are several other advertising system options, including:

- AdGenta
- Blogads
- CrispAds
- IntelliTXT.
- DoubleClick
- Kanoodle
- Text Link Ads (note the warning later in this section)

In fact, there are many types and varieties of advertising, from banners, links, and textual ads to pop-ups. It is easy to be overwhelmed and not know which to try first. The best idea is to focus your efforts on one or two at a time and take the advice of other bloggers as to what is working for them.

Although there is a great variety of advertising types, in general they fall under the following headers:

- **Banner advertising** — These are the traditional graphical ads showing text and pictures. These can be bought and served up by an advertising system or can be bought as a private deal between the advertiser and blogger. Banners have been around for a long time in Internet years so they are very familiar to web users. You can see some examples of banner ads in Figure 5-2.

**Figure 5-2:** Some example banners.

- **Textual advertising** — Textual ads do not have graphics, just text and a link. They are extremely popular with advertisers, especially when served up "contextually;" that is, when the ad is automatically matched to the content it sits next to. This makes them ultra-targeted; for example, someone searching for "red widgets" would see ads for "red widgets" in the page. Programs like AdSense and YPN are very popular with bloggers mostly because they are simple to use. Implementing this type of advertising just involves pasting some code into your templates. Everything else, from finding advertisers to showing ads, is done for you. Contextual ads best suit blogs that have some sort of commercial angle with many associated products and services being advertised. They are not so good with "general" multi-topic blogs or opinion-based subject areas. See Figure 5-3 for some example text ads.

**Figure 5-3:** Example textual ads.

- **Product-based advertising**—A recent type of ad system has arrived that aims to promote specific products from retailers or auctions. The best known of these is Chitika's eMiniMalls product. These systems, either contextually or based on the blogger's tweaking, target readers with product selections showing thumbnail images and pricing. For product-heavy niches these systems can work well, but as with all of these ad types, testing and tweaking is required. Figure 5-4 shows what these ads look like.

**Figure 5-4:** Chitika eMiniMalls.

- **Text-link ads** — For a while selling links was an increasingly popular way to sell ads. The beauty of these is that they don't take up much room, and that depending upon the system you choose to run them, you can have control over which advertisers you accept and reject. Advertisers loved the system because the links influenced Google and improved search-engine results. Many bloggers were using links as their main income generator. Unfortunately, Google made a big public fuss about its disapproval of text links, giving out penalties and driving the sales underground and scaring off many bloggers. Selling links is not something we recommend unless you are sure you know what you are doing.

- **RSS ads** — An increasingly popular way for people to read blogs is via RSS. As a result, publishers and ad providers have been keen to find ways to place ads in feeds. These attempts have been met with a variety of success levels. Though you do not hear of too many people making big dollars with RSS ads as yet, they are an area to keep aware of. Appearing as they do in the feed makes them complementary to any onsite advertising, plus it allows you to make money off the people who never visit the blog itself.

- **Sponsorships** — Another form of advertising that a smaller number of bloggers are using is sponsorship. The nature of the sponsorship can vary from deal to deal, but in most cases it consists of showing banners for a certain amount of time, showing logos in the header or sidebar, or being mentioned in competitions or reviews as being a supplier of a product.

---

**EXERCISE**

Make a note of the blogs you know that run advertising, which type, and how many ads they display. Do you find yourself distracted or put off by these ads? Which from your list do it well, and which blogs go too far?

---

## Ad Payment Types

Ads can pay for being present for a certain amount of time regardless of any other metric, such as $x per month. Then there are ads that are paid according to more strict criteria. There are three popular performance-based payment types currently in use:

- **CPC** — CPC stands for "cost per click." Payment is on a "per-click" basis, so for each click of an ad the publisher gets paid a certain amount.
- **CPM** — CPM stands for "cost per thousand" views and means the publisher gets paid a certain amount for the number of times an ad is displayed. Each display is regarded as an "impression."
- **CPA** — CPA stands for "cost per acquisition," meaning the publisher gets paid a commission if the ad makes a sale, signup, or generates a lead.

# Finding Advertisers

The advantage of automated systems is, in theory, that they bring advertisers to you, but this is not always necessarily the case, plus some of the best deals will be those you arrange yourself. For a start, there will be no middleman taking a cut.

The key to getting advertisers is to make your blog attractive, and then approach likely prospects with a good pitch.

## Preparing for Advertisers

Step one in getting advertising is to put your house in order.

### Have an "Advertise Here" Button and an Advertising Page

This is fundamental. If advertisers are going to know they can advertise on your blog, you need to show them, plus you need to have all the required information available at hand. Have an easy way to contact you for more information and your rates if they are not already visible. Make an attractive image and put it where it can be seen.

Clearly explain who you are, what your site is about, and why you are an authority on your topic. The key is to answer why anyone should care enough to purchase an ad. Answer "What's in it for me?" Darren's advertising page is shown in Figure 5-5.

### Show Them What They Will Be Buying

If you currently have no paid placements on your site, put up "house ads" (house ads are banners for products or sites from your own company) or partner ads in the same spot you would run a paid spot should it sell.

**Advertise on ProBlogger**

*Become a Premium Sponsor ProBlogger and have it seen by hundreds of thousands of web entrepreneurs and influencers.*

ProBlogger is viewed by hundreds of thousands of readers every month and is one of the few blogs around that is **almost exclusively read by bloggers**.

As a result it represents a unique opportunity for those wanting to give their product or service the chance of being sneezed quickly throughout the blogosphere in a viral manner.

Your Message Here

**Figure 5-5:** A sample "advertise here" page.

### Give a Freebie

Create a free advertisement on your site to get attention from the target company or their competitors. Politely ask for how well the ad works out (for example, total clicks, any purchases, and so on). You might find that once you start delivering traffic, the company is willing to pay for the spot to maintain the stream of new visitors.

### Show off Your Stats

You need to show at least the basic information, such as monthly unique visitors and page views. To many advertisers, traffic numbers are key. Keep working to keep these stats updated as you build traffic. Be ready to share your numbers and back them up with graphs from multiple stats packages as evidence.

Any other information that might be useful to advertisers is also well worth displaying, such as gender and age demographic information. Demonstrate that you know your audience well and appeal to their market. If you do not have this information at hand, put together a survey or pay to get more detailed stats from comScore or Quantcast.

Darren often tells potential advertisers the keywords and phrases he ranks for in Google. Compile a list of words that you rank for that you can pull out next time you're talking to an advertiser. If people search the Web for information on products that they sell and they end up on your site, you have a valuable and unique selling point.

### Keep Your Blog on Topic and Professional

If you are not writing on topics that attract a specific audience, advertisers won't know if they are a good fit for your site. Talking about random topics, ranting about your drive to work, swearing, bashing every product you can think of, and other unpredictable behavior will scare away advertisers.

### Put Together an Advertiser Pack

Not all advertisers will want to read your advertising page, plus it looks more professional to have comprehensive information available rather than a brief overview page. Compile your stats, rates, advertising options (that is, what you offer), reader demographics, and any other relevant figures into a professional-looking document that you can email to interested advertisers. Include your contact details, references, and testimonials from other advertisers if you can get them.

### Niches Sell

Most of us will never directly compete with the broad mainstream publications that are out there. Don't try to fool advertisers into thinking that you're bigger than you are; use your niche status as a positive and sell the fact that you can speak persuasively to a narrow and highly targeted group of people. This makes the money an advertiser spends much more effective: "Spend $1 on a big site, and you might reach a lot of people who are mildly interested in your topic; sell $1 on our site, and you'll reach people who are *obsessed* with your topic…"

## Getting Advertisers

Once you know your angle, the next step is to find and approach potential advertisers.

### Finding Advertisers

Start closest to home. Have a look at your own blog; are there people advertising on it already? If you have Google AdSense running on your blog, then Google is already serving up advertisers for you. Why not contact them and do a deal?

Next, check out who is advertising on blogs similar to yours. Click on a few and find the contact details. Send a polite and brief email asking if they'd be interested in advertising on your blog as well. Include brief information to get them interested, along with a link to your advertise page, and mention your advertiser pack without sending it to them right away.

Companies that already advertise on blogs are going to be a lot more open to advertising on yours than companies who have not yet tried this kind of advertising. But by the same logic, those who are already advertising online will be more likely to try advertising on blogs than those who do not yet do any web advertising. Look to see who is buying Google AdWords for your common niche searches.

You will know the products and companies in your niche. Make a wish list of every company you would love to see advertising on your blog, and start contacting them. In the end, selling advertising is a numbers game, and the more frogs you kiss, the better chances you have of turning up a prince.

## Approaching Advertisers

Whereas some advertisers will contact you after reading your "advertise here" page, you'll need to directly approach the rest of them, so it is a good idea to create a standard letter to contact the advertisers. There is no one size fits all solution here, but you can follow these general guidelines:

1. Introduce yourself and quickly explain why you are emailing them.
2. Explain why you chose to contact them, with an emphasis on what *they* have to gain.
3. Give brief details about your blog (traffic, subscribers, topic, audience).
4. Tell them about the advertising options (location on the site, max number of advertisers, monthly price).

Do not overdo it. Potential advertisers should be able to decide pretty quickly if they are interested or not. If they reply, then you can fill in all the fine details. Keep in mind that all the information I mentioned should be contained in two or three paragraphs, tops. If you send an essay to potential advertisers, they will just trash it as spam.

**EXERCISE**

Brainstorm potential advertisers who might be interested in your blog. As you go around reading blogs, also take a note of who is advertising and from the "advertise here" pages, what they might be paying. Are there any "likely suspects" who tend to advertise a lot? What are the going rates in your niche?

## Taking Payments

You might have everything else in place, but if you are not able to take payments or, more importantly, if advertisers are not able to pay *easily*, you will end up losing deals.

PayPal is generally the best option, because it allows you to accept cash transfers and credit card payments; however, PayPal is not currently available in all countries.

## How Much to Charge

How much you should charge depends on what an advertiser would expect to pay and how much value you provide.

Advertisers, of course, will want to see a return for their investment. This might be in the form of sales increase or increased exposure. Make sure, therefore, that you do everything in your power to ensure your blog demonstrably delivers.

Remember that there are some pretty cheap advertising options out there and you will need to be competitive. Provided you reserved a good spot for the sponsors (sidebar or header, preferably) you could start by charging $0.50 CPM (50 cents per 1,000 page views). With this pricing, a blog generating 100,000 monthly page views would earn around $50 a month for that one advert.

Start low to attract early sales and then build your prices steadily upward. Super-popular blogs such as TechCrunch have earned a higher CPM, sometimes as high as $10, but it takes time and a great deal of credibility to get there.

You can easily check whether you are charging a suitable rate by using AdSense units on the places where you will sell direct advertising. Analyze how much you would gain with AdSense, and adjust your rates accordingly. Secondly, you can also check similar sites' "advertise here" pages.

Be flexible regarding the terms, perhaps even offering free test periods. Make advertising agreements on a month-to-month basis. People don't like to commit to something they are not completely confident in. Encourage longer-term deals with a discount.

## Ad Formats

Which ad formats to show is probably mostly a question of what advertisers are willing to pay for! If you look around, though, most bloggers are using the small, square, 125-pixel banner size like Darren's, shown in Figure 5-2 earlier in this chapter.

Over the past year or so the 125-by-125-pixel advertisement has emerged as the most common size for advertisements. Some of the more prominent blogs using these small square ads include TechCrunch, ReadWriteWeb, Copyblogger, John Chow dot Com, as well as many others.

The 125-by-125-pixel ads are an attractive option for bloggers and advertisers for the following reasons:

- Blog designers like the way they fit nicely into sidebars in a square or vertical line.
- They give the option to sell multiple ad units in a space often reserved for one larger ad (four 125-by-125 ads fit nicely into either the position of a skyscraper or a large rectangular ad). This provides options and also potentially more revenue.
- Advertisers like the fact that they are often cheaper than a larger ad so they can have their ad appear on multiple blogs for the same price as one larger one on a single blog.
- Affiliate programs are more and more offering publishers 125-by-125-pixel ads to promote their products. We look at affiliate programs in detail later. Bloggers can use these in their unsold ad spots, making good use of their space and making their ads look more popular.

Some ad formats work better in some industries than others; each niche and industry will have its own preferences for ad unit sizes. Many larger advertisers will have ad agencies on their payroll that might prefer more traditional ad sizes, and some are not set up to sell anything else.

The best idea is to look around to see what ad types sell well in your niche before deciding which types you should offer.

## How Many Ads to Display

Before filling your blog with ads, consider the effect having too many ads can cause.

Displaying too many ads is bad for readers because having too many ads can crowd out the content and put off new visitors to your blog. Some blogs have so many ads that their content is pushed way down the page and effectively hidden.

From an advertiser's point of view, too many ads on a page dilutes the conversion that advertisers get. If an ad is one of 4 they have a much higher chance of being noticed and clicked on than if the ad is one of 10.

Look around your niche to see where blogs place ads and how many. Take particular note of any that seem "overdone." In most cases you will see an ad in the header, and maybe four or so small ads in a sidebar. Much more than that, and your blog risks looking more like a racing car than a content site.

## Optimizing Advertising

To get the best performance out of your advertising, you need to have advertising where it can be seen without causing annoyance and distracting from the content. This means balancing highly visible placements and ad formats against your regular readers' comfort.

In general this means putting ads "above the fold;" that is, above the bottom of the browser window, where you wouldn't need to scroll to see it. Ads tend to get more clicks if they are embedded in content, but make sure they do not obstruct legibility.

With services like Google AdSense, you can test color variations, and it is well worth experimenting. Some bloggers do well with ads that are blended into the color scheme of their blog, and others say they get better results when ads stand out and contrast with the rest of their content. Ideally, though you might get more clicks, camouflaging ads as navigation is a pretty crummy trick to play on your readers and might even get you into trouble with the ad service.

Monitor any changes you make to see if you improve performance or reduce it, and get advice from other bloggers about what works for them.

## Other Direct Forms of Income

In addition to advertising, there are a few other ways to make direct income. Let's take a look at some now.

### Affiliate Programs

Affiliate programs are where you take a commission for referring a customer of a product. Probably the most common of these for bloggers is the Amazon Associates program that now has tens of thousands of products that you can link to. Darren uses it to great effect on his photography blog (see Figure 5-6). Other affiliate programs that represent many different companies and products include LinkShare, Commission Junction, and ClickBank.

---

**Digital SLRs**

1. Canon Digital Rebel XT 8MP Digital SLR Camera with EF-S 18-55mm f3.5-5.6 Lens
2. Canon Digital Rebel XTi 10.1MP Digital SLR Camera (Black Body Only)
3. Nikon D200 10.2MP Digital SLR Camera (Body Only)
4. Canon EOS 30D 8.2MP Digital SLR Camera (Body Only)
5. Nikon D40x 10.2MP
6. Nikon D80 10.2MP Digital SLR Camera Kit with 18-135mm
7. Pentax K10D 10.2MP Digital SLR Camera with Shake Reduction (Body Only)
8. Sony Alpha A100K 10.2MP Digital SLR Camera Kit with 18-70mm
9. Canon EOS 5D 12.8 MP Digital SLR Camera (Body Only)
10. Nikon D50 6.1MP Digital SLR Camera (Body Only)

---

**Figure 5-6:** Darren uses Amazon links on his photography blog.

**EXERCISE**

List good-quality products that you have bought recently that match your niche. Sign up to Amazon Associates so you can provide links to them. Search the top blogs in your subject and related areas for reviews to get an idea of the products you could feature on your blog.

# Tips for Using Affiliate Programs on Your Blog

Affiliate programs take some work if you want to get the most out of them, but can be lucrative if you match the right program with the right blog/topic.

You must be careful when using affiliate links, because in effect you are recommending a product. Suggest your readers purchase a lousy or disreputable product and expect to lose your good reputation very quickly. Also the FTC in the USA has strict rules governing affiliates. For a start you need to disclose your affiliate relationship and be careful about any claims you make about a product's performance.

Here are some tips for getting the most out of affiliate marketing on your blog.

## Consider Your Audience

Put yourself in your readers' shoes and consider what they might be looking for as they surf by your blog. Are they shopping for specific products? Might they be looking for related products or accessories? What would trigger them to purchase? Start with your reader in mind rather than the product. If you take this approach you could end up doing your reader a favor as well as making a few dollars on the side.

## Authenticity

There are literally hundreds of thousands of products and services for you to choose from to recommend to your readers, but making money from them is not as simple as randomly adding links to them from your blog. Readers come back to your blog day after day because something about you resonates with them. Don't recommend products you don't fully believe will benefit them. If you have doubts, say so.

The best results I've had from affiliate programs are where I give an open and honest appraisal of the product, including both its strengths and weaknesses. You might think that this isn't a wise move and that to make maximum sales you should give every product a glowing review; however, sales consistently prove otherwise. People want to know what they are buying. Consider your own experience of shopping at Amazon or anywhere else that displays reviews.

Wherever possible, choose products and companies with a good reputation and quality sales pages.

## Link Deep

We always say to bloggers that we're consulting with that they should learn something from contextual advertising when it comes to affiliate programs. The secret of contextual ads like AdSense is that the advertisements match the content. The same is true for affiliate programs. A banner to a general page on every page on your site won't be anywhere near as effective as multiple links throughout your blog that advertise products that are relevant.

So if you're writing an MP3 player review, link directly to a page selling that particular product.

## Traffic Is Important

Although it's not the *only* factor, traffic levels are key when it comes to making money from affiliate marketing. The more people who see your affiliate links, the more likely you will be to make a sale. Consider how you might direct traffic on your blog toward pages where they are more likely to see your affiliate links.

## Track Results

Most affiliate programs have at least some type of tracking. See what is selling and what isn't. Watching your results can help you plan future affiliate efforts. Keep track of what positions for links work well, which products sell, what wording around links works well, and so on, and use the information that you collect as you plan future affiliate strategies.

> **PROBLOGGER BLOG TIP: AFFILIATE LINKS**
>
> There has been a lot of debate over the years about affiliate links, but in general, if you link to a product you genuinely would recommend regardless of any commission, I don't think you will go far wrong. In reviews now, people expect to be pointed to a place where a product can be bought. Where your audience is particularly sensitive, you might want to draw attention in the post that although your links go through your affiliate link you would recommend the product either way, and provide a general disclaimer in your footer or about page.

## Donations

Rather than sell something via ads or affiliates, you can ask for small donations. A very small number of blogs have a history of making good money with donations — Jason Kottke and Leo Laporte come to mind.

To be successful with asking for money from readers you'll want to have a large and loyal readership that gets a lot of value from your work. Most bloggers just don't have the critical mass or the cult following to make it work very well, but you could make a few dollars.

I once experimented with a "Buy Me a Coffee" button. Although I never disclose my earnings out of principle, I did get a bunch of donations through the plugin. It averaged out to a few donations every couple of days after the initial spike. Providing you write posts that people like to reward, I can see donations competing income-wise with AdSense.

Although I did not take the donations route for long, here are my findings:

- People are willing to reward bloggers when they see value in your writing.
- There seemed to be some pent-up demand for a concrete way my readers could thank me. For this reason alone it might have been worth keeping it or finding some other outlet for gratitude.

- A lot of the notice it was given might be due to novelty; there was a big batch at the beginning, but that trailed off.
- My most rewarded posts were the motivational kind. There seems to be a correlation between donations and "feeling good," which makes sense to me. On the other hand, the messages I received imply it was people who had been reading for a while who donated, so the blog as a whole matters as much as the single post they clicked through from.
- People have judged it as "begging." I don't see it that way, but your readers might. The majority of people who sent me money were genuinely grateful for what they had read.
- You can't get better encouragement than someone sending you money out of their own pocket! If somebody gives you cash, you know you are on the right track somewhere.
- It's useful to have a PayPal button around your blog — a couple of people used it to send me unrelated payments.

Sounds good, right? So why did I not leave it up?

For me it was just a matter of taste. I would encourage anyone who is interested to try it, but for my own blog I don't think donations work because I make sufficient income from my products and services.

## Classifieds

Some blogs do very well out of classifieds, such as Darren's ProBlogger Job Board (http://jobs.problogger.net; see Figure 5-7). If you have a sizable audience that needs to advertise jobs, personals, sales, or want ads, then it might be worth a try.

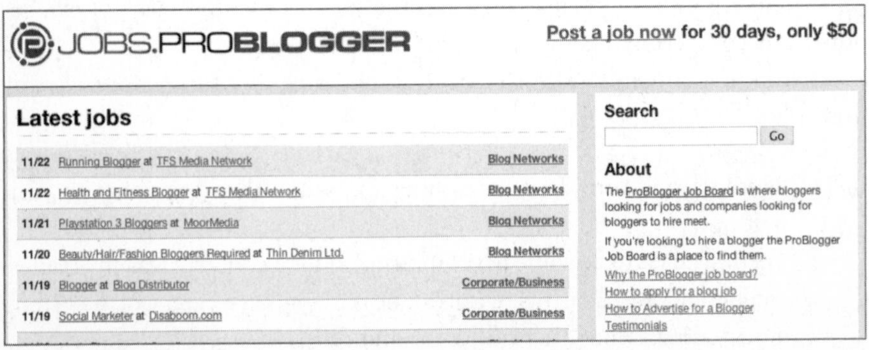

**Figure 5-7:** The ProBlogger Job Board.

## Merchandise

This will not work for every blog, but there are services out there such as CafePress.com that allow you to create merchandise like T-shirts, mugs, and so on with your own logos and designs. With the right topic and/or audience you might sell well, with the added benefit of each customer acting like a walking billboard for your blog.

## Subscriptions

One of my favorite monetization strategies is anything that allows you to charge a subscription rather than a one-off payment. Make a sale once but get paid over and over. It's the gym membership model.

Some bloggers do this with private forums, like Darren's `http://problogger.com` membership site, while others offer online training courses, like Chris' `http://AuthorityBlogger.com` course. It's well worth investigating.

The problem that some bloggers face is that some of the topics that you could think to start a membership site about already have free content available. To make it succeed you must have some sort of premium/exclusive content and/or real expertise on your topic.

# Indirect Income-Earning Strategies

Rather than work to make money from advertising and other direct means, another profitable blogging route is to make money indirectly. Indirect monetization tactics rely on you demonstrating your experience, expertise, and personality through your blog. Let's take a look at the popular indirect monetization options.

## Freelance Blogging

Freelance blogging is a great way to earn money from blogs. Rather than working on your own blog in order to make money from advertising, people are willing to pay to have someone blog on their behalf.

Though it isn't a passive income, it does earn reasonably well, predictably, and is itself a form of marketing, so doing a good job often leads to more work.

When starting out, you might have to start at the lower end of the pay scale — $10 a post is quite common — but as you build a reputation you can earn more than 10 times that amount.

It's not just about the money; it is also a lot of fun, especially if you enjoy writing and variety. I started out very much in the technical and geeky topics, but now I find myself writing about all sorts of things, from clients as diverse as a micro stock photography company to a software developer. I am in a lucky position that these jobs now come to me; in the past that was not always the case.

The first place to start looking for writing jobs is with your own blog and your own audience. Put up a page saying you are available for hire and refer to it in your sidebar and posts. Those people who read your writing regularly are the most likely to want to hire you, because they already know and like your work and there is some trust built up. You are a known quantity.

By extension, any guest posting you do has the same potential. Though readers will not see you as often, putting a small reference to your freelance availability in your attribution line could garner some leads. See if you can get some guest-post spots on likely blogs, and try.

Next, ask around. Work outward from your blog to people who know you. Put the word out that you are looking for writing work. This isn't begging; you can really help someone else with your writing skills or just by saving them time. Friends of friends and word of mouth is where I get half my work, so this is a really effective method. When you are down it is hard to sell yourself, so it really helps if someone is doing it for you.

Work the forums. Your writing doesn't have to appear only on blogs to get noticed; blogging forums are also a good place to get your name out there. Good forum posts and a friendly, helpful nature could be all you need to get either paid work or guest spots that lead to paid work. As before, mention in your profile your availability.

Apply to online job ads. There are lots of online job boards; you can start at the following locations:

```
http://freelancewritinggigs.com
http://jobs.problogger.net
http://craigslist.org
http://jobs.freelanceswitch.com
```

Once you get word out and really start looking, you will see there are writing opportunities all over for a hard-working blogger.

## What Blog Owners Look For

There are many reasons someone might hire a blogger, but the most common are listed here:

- To increase traffic, visibility, and search-engine rankings
- To build credibility and authority
- To supply constant content to keep visitors returning
- To increase sales leads and repeat customers

When site owners are looking for a blogger to write for them, they have the following criteria in mind:

- Can they write original and interesting articles for the topic?
- Does their style suit the property and audience?
- Are they able to write all required types of content?
- Will I get more value back than what I pay out?

The first three points all cover the craft of writing. If you can show ability in your writing samples, the job of getting the gig is half done. Usually, though, there are several other writers in the running, so the last point is where the choice is really made.

If you are looking to get paid blog-writing gigs you have to have a good archive of posts that you can point to, plus evidence of value over and above just the writing. Here are some tips:

- Create your own blog; demonstrate you can do the job that needs filling.
- Vary your standard posts to show off your capabilities. Have a collection of newsy posts, review posts, opinion posts, essays, and tutorials. If there is a certain blog you want to write for, try to match exactly the sort of content they like, their style, and tone of voice.
- Show you have high-value skills such as basic SEO and promotional experience.
- Get known in forums. With intelligent blog comments, people are more likely to hire you if they know who you are.

The question to ask is, "Why me? Why would someone select me over some other blogger?" If you can answer that convincingly, you will have no trouble getting paid blogging gigs.

## Why Freelance Blogging?

For the blogger the benefits come down to increased exposure and pay. Payment can be per-post, word-count-based, or on a retainer. Obviously, all fees come down to negotiation, expectations, article length, complexity, and blogger experience. If you are just starting out, do not expect to get more than $20 a post, but for a proven blogger in a competitive niche, with lots of research required, you can earn 10 or 20 times that amount.

The arrangement can work very well for both the blogger and the client providing everything is clear from the start, and the responsibility for making sure this happens is on the blogger.

Some example questions you might need to agree on beforehand are as follows:

- Who is in charge and what is their goal?
- How will the goals be measured?
- Will your performance affect the contract?
- Which topics should be covered?
- Are there verboten topics?
- What is the schedule?
- Will you email copy or post it live yourself?
- How will you be paid and when?
- Will it be a fixed-term or rolling contract?
- Who owns the content?
- Are you being paid just to write or will there be other tasks?
- Do they have a stock photography account or will you have to supply images?

Normally all this can be cleared up with a single conversation, but it's always best to get these things in writing.

## Magazines and Books

Once you make a bit of a name for yourself online, you can use this experience and reputation to get jobs and contracts writing for print. It's about being seen as an expert in your field and having something original to say.

You will find publishers are more receptive to having an idea pitched to them by someone who has already managed to gather an audience, and they might even seek you out.

This book you are reading right now came about because of one particular popular blog!

Many blogs already have large amounts of content ready to be pulled together into a book. It isn't only publishers who are looking out for writers; sometimes already-signed authors get bogged down trying to complete their own book or need a gap in their expertise filled. After Chris's technical articles became popular he was approached on several occasions to join authors to collaborate on books that wouldn't have been completed otherwise.

Although books obviously provide more prestige, magazines and newspapers work on a faster schedule and can be just as lucrative, or on occasion more so. To land these gigs, email editors for their submission guidelines. Again, like books, sometimes the work comes to you. Manolo from Manolo's Shoe Blog landed a writing gig in *The Washington Post Express* after he was discovered via his blog.

## Speaking

Once again this is dependent upon the topic you're writing about, but some bloggers end up with all kinds of opportunities to speak at conferences, workshops, and seminars on their topic of choice. Sometimes they are freebies, other times the conference will cover costs, and on other occasions there are speakers' fees. If you are lucky, you might even have an opportunity to hear both Darren and me at various conferences!

## Consulting

When you are perceived as an expert on a topic, you will find that people naturally come to you for advice and some of them are willing to pay for it. A good deal of my income is from consulting work and I am fortunate that this work comes to me rather than having to go out and sell it.

Some niches are probably better positioned than others for their bloggers to get into paid consultancy work, of course. The key is to demonstrate expertise and experience every day in your blog and to build trust. If you show that you are reliable and can help, you have won half the battle.

Potential customers will not know you have services to offer unless you tell them. I have a banner in my sidebar that leads to a services page showing example offerings along with pricing. You can see this in Figure 5-8. A particularly nice bonus for me is anyone buying, say, an hour phone consultancy, will pay in advance through a PayPal button, meaning I get far fewer non-paying customers now.

**Figure 5-8:** Chris's services banner.

---

**PROBLOGGER BLOG TIP: SELL YOUR SERVICES**

Could you make some money selling your own services? Many people overlook marketable skills and experience they have developed. It's not just writers, designers, and programmers who can benefit from providing work this way. Things you do every day might be just the solution someone is looking for. In fact, once you have your own blog up and running, you might find people want to know if you can help them do the same thing! Take some time to think of possible services you can offer.

---

## Employment Opportunities

Even if you are not a freelancer, blogging can be an excellent addition to your resume. If you can demonstrate expertise and experience you could get hired by your dream employer. PR blogger Steve Rubel was hired by a bigger PR firm. We have to believe the job was offered because of the profile he'd built from blogging. Bloggers are increasingly being targeted by companies because of their demonstrated abilities in their field of expertise. Of course, bloggers have also lost their jobs because of what they had written!

## Selling e-Resources

I wasn't sure whether to classify this as direct or indirect (and depending upon how you do it you could probably go either way), but some bloggers are leveraging the expertise they have in an area by putting together their own "e-products" such as e-books, online courses, and videos.

Darren has sold ebooks from both his Problogger and Digital Photography School blogs, and Chris sells ebooks directly to his chrisg.com audience, and also through third-party collaborations, such as Wordtracker.

Chris also runs courses, such as his Authority Blogger online course, and also teleseminar and webinar based courses where you can hear and interact with him live.

The key to selling digital products is to attract an audience with a clear want or need and to solve their challenges. You will find it much tougher to write your ebook or course and then try to find a market for it!

You can see examples of ebooks in the Problogger Book Member Download Area:

```
http://probloggerbook.com/bonus/
```

If you have not already, sign up here: (Make sure you type the address exactly as shown.)

```
http://probloggerbook.com/?/register/bonus
```

## Networking and Business Partnerships

One of the benefits of blogging about a niche topic that interests you is that you will begin to connect with others who have similar interests and expertise. As you interact with them, it's amazing to see the opportunities for working together that arise.

## Summary

Both Darren and I make money from blogging in our own ways. We are living examples that it is possible to not only make a good living, but also have fun doing it!

Whichever way you choose — direct, indirect, or a mixture — I hope this chapter offers an approach to making money by blogging that is right for you.

# 6

# Buying and Selling Blogs

Over the past couple of years, we have seen some high-profile blogs changing hands for some tidy sums of money — upwards of five figures for well-known properties.

It started with domains and traditional websites, but now blogs are carving a market unique to website sales.

The most publicized sale probably was that of Blog Herald (Figure 6-1), which has been bought and sold a couple of times. One of the blogs I helped found, Performancing, also attracted a lot of attention and speculation when it changed hands in early 2007.

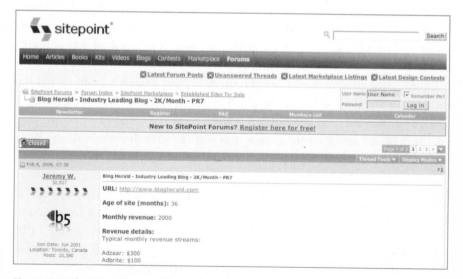

**Figure 6-1:** Blog Herald created buzz when it sold.

Though the sums involved often surprise a lot of people outside of blogging, once you start thinking of blogs as a business asset it is easy to understand how they will start to become traded as such.

As more people hear about the money being made, of course they are piling in to see if they can get their share, too. This chapter is all about how you, too, can buy and sell blogs for profit.

# Introduction to Buying and Selling Blogs

Buying and selling blogs is like any form of property trading. You have buyers, sellers, brokers, and even people who buy to sell (flip) online properties. Just like buying and selling physical property, there are risks, scams, and fraudsters too, so do your research before getting involved.

## Why Sell?

The first question we have to address is why someone would sell a blog they have put so much effort into building up.

As you might expect, the most common reason is profit. People are willing to pay good money for a well-developed blog. In fact, you can get fair money for a not-so-well-developed blog as a fixer-upper! There are a growing number of people using blog sales as their primary source of professional blogging income.

A lot of the private sales I've been privy to have been where an owner has been made an offer too good to turn down, but there are also many cases where the owner needed cash and needed it fast.

What about cases where money was not the primary motivation? Well, there's a percentage of bloggers who try it for a while until they decide one day it is all just too hard. Some just give up, others try to recoup some compensation for the time and money they have sunk, and some don't want to see the blog go to waste. Take my photography blog, DSLRBlog, for example. I started the blog with the intention of learning photography, which I did, but I soon found it was becoming hard work to keep it running. My friends who were initially helping me with it lost interest. One day I was made a very healthy offer, which I joyfully accepted. It is sad to see someone take what you have built and change it in unrecognizable ways, but it is better than leaving something to rot that you put so much work into.

When you set out to start a blog, you think it will go on forever, but as we all know, life has a habit of changing. What with families, careers, businesses, and so on, all it takes is one event to change your mind and priorities. It doesn't have to particularly be a catastrophe; it could be a job offer or a new baby. Not many people would choose to continue to blog over such commitments!

Bragging rights also come into it. What would you prefer as a story: "I tried and failed," or, "I built it and sold it"?

Whatever your reason, selling your blog is probably the more financially prudent exit strategy compared to not renewing your hosting fees and letting the blog fade away.

# Why Buy?

We can understand someone selling a blog; it seems perfectly reasonable. There are two parties to a transaction, though. Why would someone buy a blog rather than start a new blog of their own?

## Advantages of Buying a Blog

There are many advantages to buying a blog rather than building one. The main advantage is time. Starting a blog and building up traffic and an audience takes a lot of time and effort; a purchase is probably the only practical shortcut available.

Buying gives you a head start, especially if you are entering a market with a lot of tough competition. Though there are instances of blogs gaining traction very quickly, none can compete with the immediate effect of taking ownership of a mature property.

Traffic, even with the best techniques, takes time and skill to grow and attract. You can buy traffic, through advertising and paying consultants, but you can find that an existing blog might have ideal traffic already and at a more affordable price.

When you are buying a mature blog, in addition to the obvious assets such as design, programming, and subscribers, what you are also buying is a proven concept. Research has been done for you, and you already have an indication of how successful the blog will be.

What you also might be buying is potential. Just like in housing deals, people buy blogs in order to refurbish them and sell them at a profit.

Having said all that, much like when looking at offline franchises, you might want to buy a blog that turns a predictable profit, where everything has already been worked out, and you just want to keep it running and reap the benefits.

### Disadvantages of Buying a Blog

Although there are many benefits, buying an existing blog is not always entirely free of problems.

First of all, of course, there is the cost. Starting a blog is cheap, and buying a blog can be expensive. If you look at just dollar value there would be no competition; you have to look at it as an investment. Like all investments, value can go up or down, and history is not always a reliable indicator of future performance.

Even with the best deal, you might be starting over with an existing audience. How this goes depends on your approach and how open-minded the readers are. Blog subscribers do not always take to new writers; after all, the new guy is not who they signed on to read.

Loyalty here is both a boon and a bane; it is hard-won and easily lost. In many cases it is a good idea to keep the old writer(s) on long enough to transition, or longer if you can work out a deal all parties are happy with. It helps everyone, not just the audience, adjust and settle in.

In most financial deals there is an element of risk. Will it all go wrong? What happens if you buy something broken or misrepresented? Could the seller run off with your money? All you can do is try to mitigate any risks you identify, and these worries put a lot of people off trying.

Research is key. Look into the seller and the site. Just like a car, a blog has many interdependent moving parts. Knowing how they work is essential, or at least knowing an expert who will help you. On the surface everything could look nice and shiny, while under the hood there could be problems. Getting third and fourth opinions could pay dividends, but you never truly know what you have bought until it is yours.

## Deciding to Build or Buy

Whether you build or buy usually comes down to a combination of three things:

- **Resources** — How much time and money do you have at your disposal? If you have all the time in the world, you can save your money and do things yourself. On the other hand, if you are up against a deadline you will have to spend money to save time.

- **Expertise** — Do you have the experience and expertise on hand to make a successful blog? Can you take the risk of getting it wrong? The only proven blog is an old blog, and the only way to get an old blog for most people is to buy one.
- **Control** — This might seem a strange thought, but it does have a big impact on people in quite surprising ways. When you buy any site, you are inheriting a lot more than bits and bytes. Your only chance to make something entirely your own is to build it yourself. If you buy a blog, you buy its baggage too. Buyers, just like when buying a pre-owned home, have to be prepared to do some work to make it feel like theirs and also be prepared to be routinely compared against the old owner.

# Buying to Sell (Flipping)

As already mentioned, a growing number of professional bloggers are looking to blog sales as a way to earn a profit. The income can be very good, plus many bloggers are more enthusiastic at launch than they are when in maintenance mode, so they can be continually working on new or refurbished blogs with full enjoyment and then offload them when they begin running out of steam.

The key to making money from buying blogs to sell is simple: *Have a market of likely buyers before you buy a blog to flip.*

At first this might not make sense, but think of the alternative. Do you want to put the time, money, and effort into a purchase only to find there are no buyers? That is a surefire way to lose on any deal. No, you need to know that if you can do a good job, you are certain to find a buyer.

Before getting into the buying-to-sell game, routinely review the buying and selling sites to see what types of blogs tend to do well and which find fewer bids. What characteristics stand out to bidders in your niche? How are the sales publicized and where? Your niche will have its own trends and habits, so get to know the winning formula for your favorite topics.

Who are the likely candidates for a blog purchase?

- Competitors
- Companies in your niche that are looking for traffic or growth
- Bloggers looking to expand their audience
- Losing bidders at a similar auction

Taxes are a potential minefield, so definitely get advice. In fact, even if there were no risk of getting into any financial trouble, you would find it useful to get an accountant's take because you might find they can help.

Always deal with the decision maker when buying or selling to make a profit, usually the CEO or owner. When buying and selling blogs as a business, you can't afford to be messed around by people who are just testing the waters or who have no authority to make a deal. Time is very much money.

---

**PROBLOGGER BLOG TIP: BUILD A BUSINESS MINDSET**

The skills in evaluating blog values are useful regardless of whether you want to actually get into buying and selling. Those bloggers who train up their business brain tend to do better overall because they have the ability to see their efforts both in terms of building an asset and creating an audience and content.

---

# Blog Sales Basics

The basic theories behind buying or selling a blog are a lot like buying or selling any property, but blogs probably have most in common with business sales or investing because there is the value in the property itself and then there is the revenue potential.

Both buyer and seller need to make an analysis of the value they perceive in the blog. What inherent value does it hold right now? What value *could* it hold?

Value can be found in the money it generates, the content that has been created, the traffic it attracts, any resale value, and the potential it holds.

In general, the older the blog is the more attractive it will be, not only because older sites are more favored in SEO circles, but also because an older blog shows history. You would hope that a blog that has been around a while has hit on a good formula and will have lower risk going forward. With all the ups and downs in search engines and blog reputations, any blog that has stood the test of time and grown an audience is a premium over blogs that are new and have unknown quantities.

When looking at an older blog, the main things to check out are stability and trends. In general, you want to see steady audience, content, and traffic growth. Be wary of random spikes and dips; these point to risky or erratic behavior. Also be aware that, just like with cars, a blog that has had one careful owner is a better gamble than a blog that has changed hands a lot.

Young blogs under, say, six months old can be bargains, but their lack of track record makes them much more of a risk. They are easier to pump up to look like a good buy when in fact they have little substance or value. In a new blog you are better off looking at the value purely in the assets, such as design, domain, and technology. The rest is too easy to game.

Go into any deal knowing your overall game plan. Will you buy to hold or buy to flip? Are you looking for monthly income, an income you can improve, or just to make money on the sale itself? Each variation will have differing tactics; for example, if you are looking to flip, you need to be more aggressive in gaining a lower purchase price and be absolutely sure you can add value. As the saying goes, "You profit when you buy, not when you sell."

In any case, don't buy at the height of a blog's value; you *sell* at the peak. Work out how much more you could make by adding value both when buying and selling, but do not allow this to cloud your mind when it comes to gaining a discount.

When you are looking at large amounts, consider using escrow. Much as you want to keep things friendly, do you really want to risk a lot of money on someone you don't know?

The first step when buying or selling is to work out how much the blog in question is worth.

## Valuations

How you arrive at a valuation is very important. You can count on it that the other party or parties will value the same blog very differently. This is not just because they will take a different approach, but because valuations are subjective and also largely depend on what you are in the deal to achieve. The same blog being bought for monthly income will attract a different price, too, if it is being bought just for the domain, or as a refurb, and so on.

There is no single standard way to value any site. Just like when valuing a business, the most common valuation method is based on a multiple of monthly income while taking other factors into account.

Even if you don't want to sell right away, you should still value your blog. Bloggers often want to know value for ego purposes too—it is a way to score yourself and compare against other blogs in your niche for sport!

## Audience

Audiences and niches are important to a valuation. If your audience is super-targeted and high-value, full of rich people who spend a lot, your blog will garner a higher price than if you have a small unidentifiable audience of freebie hunters.

Registered users, email subscribers, well-frequented forums, and RSS counts have high value. In fact, email lists can be sold off separately. Loyal, engaged users are extremely sought-after.

Even related niche audiences still vary in value. For example, "make money" and "blogging" niches might be overlapping, but you can make more profit from people who are looking to make money than from the general "blogging" audience. Knowing which niches will return higher revenue is important in deciding which blogs are a good buy.

## Content

Every blog needs good content; that is a given. It is hardly worth buying an empty blog unless you particularly like the domain, template, or some special technology. If that is the case, you might be better off hiring a freelancer. When purchasing a blog, you need to look at the whole package; when selling, you need to make that package as attractive as possible.

Great content is expensive no matter how you look at it, in terms of talent, ideas, time, or money. Therefore, content should have value. Pinning down a dollar value, though, is very hard to do. My approach is to consider how much effort it would be to create and what results the content is currently achieving; for example, a simple "me-too" article versus something remarkable that gains hundreds of links and visitors.

Due to the fact there are many freelancers willing to work for pennies, content is often seen by some as a commodity. This is simply not true; great content is worth a premium because it is what your visitors will be coming to see.

If you have to choose between quantity and quality, go for the latter. It always makes me wonder why sites containing millions of "computer-generated" pages (that is, spam) still sell; 1,000,000 x $0 = $0!

Where the content was acquired is as important as the quality. You need to know you have ownership of what you are buying. Do not even consider buying a blog if you even suspect there are plagiarized, automated, or free or private-label articles. A blog full of stolen or duplicate content is too much of a liability to be worth it.

Often overlooked in the excitement of buying a blog is where the new content will come from. Can you write well on the topic? Will the existing bloggers stay on? How much will you need to pay them? Can you find replacement bloggers? All these questions and more need to be answered.

## Search Rankings

Companies will often buy blogs that rank for phrases that are important to them. It is often more cost-effective than other solutions.

How can a blog at several thousand dollars be more cost-effective than ranking their own site? Well, for a start you get instant and guaranteed results, but secondly, a red-hot SEO expert would probably pay me several thousand dollars in consultancy fees, and more than likely a large amount on an ongoing basis.

If a company buys a blog that ranks on the same page as its own site, the company will then get two search results, thereby doubling the chances of a click.

Although a top ranking on Google is often listed as a selling point, you do have to consider whether that result is worth anything *to you*. In SEO circles there are search results, and then there are *valuable* search results. Valuable rankings are often called search rankings for "money terms" — that is, phrases worth money. A result that never gathers any clicks is not worth considering.

Never buy a blog because it "ranks for many phrases." This is meaningless unless those keywords are much sought-after. Bottom line, a search phrase is useful only if (A) people actually search using those keywords and (B) you can do something valuable with the traffic.

## Traffic

A blog that attracts thousands of visitors month after month is extremely valuable. You want long-term, verifiable traffic, diversified, from a reliable source.

Ideally you want a lot of traffic, from many sources and spread over several places on your blog. A single source or a single hero article increases the risk that your traffic might dry up or be fake.

Note I did not say you want just "traffic." Sellers will inflate their traffic figures. Sometimes traffic is misleading because of the way the stats are gathered or because they have been pumping the traffic artificially.

You need to see reliable stats, not their log analysis. If the only stats available are from logs, get a copy of the logs and analyze them yourself. When in serious negotiation, ask if you can put your Google Analytics code into the blog so you can watch traffic yourself.

Digg spikes (see Figure 6-2) should be separated out from your calculations. Very often you will see blogs listed with "20,000 unique visitors a month" only to find 19,990 of those unique visitors came directly from Digg and will never visit again and will not subscribe or take any other action. Digg hits are worth having in the future and when done right, but past spikes should not be taken into account in your valuation. If visitors are blog nourishment, Digg spikes are empty calories!

In addition to sustained and diverse traffic, you want to look for blogs with targeted traffic. Non-targeted traffic has fewer monetization options; in fact, the main choice is impression-based ads, whereas there is a world of opportunity when the traffic is targeted.

Paid traffic, though not as attractive as free, is not a bad thing provided the blog still turns a profit and you get all the required details, deals, and permissions for it to continue.

If you are on the selling side, keep this in mind. High traffic levels are a selling point, but only if your buyer can believe you.

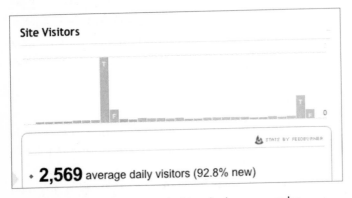

**Figure 6-2:** Traffic spikes can make blogs look more popular.

## Inbound Links

Many blogs that are bought for SEO benefits are purchased simply for the inbound links they have attracted. A good spread of quality natural links, featuring no link-farmed, fake, or bought links, is a valuable prospect. Aim for both deep links and links pointed at the homepage, with varied and well-targeted anchor text. Essentially, find blogs that search engines would favor.

## Brand

Branding can work both in your favor and against you. A respected and famous brand can be worth a lot of money, but readers might also be loyal to the old owner, or the brand might have peaked, with no room for improvement.

Is the blog a draw because of the archive of useful content or because of the blogger's personality?

If you are selling, carefully cultivate the brand awareness, and long before you put it up for sale, recruit fellow bloggers and depersonalize. That way the changeover will not be such an audience shock.

## Profit

If the blog shows a profit, this will get the most attention. Profit is both directly and obviously valuable, but it is also a proxy metric for other signs of quality; after all, a blog with zero visitors or content is not going to make a great profit!

Under no circumstances should you take revenue figures; you need to split the profit out to know that you are not taking on a liability. Only profit makes sense, unless you are happy to buy a blog laden with debt, advertising costs, and no way of paying you back!

After determining the level of profit, you need to determine the following:

- How hard is that profit to earn?
- Can *you* earn that?
- Where does the profit come from?
- How have profits changed over time? (Get a monthly breakdown.)
- How easy would it be to grow that profit?
- What other potential products and revenue sources are there?

Just like with traffic, you want the income to be diversified, easy to work, and not reliant on any "special deals" that would be lost with change of ownership. Given a choice between a blog that makes money with various advertising channels and only one or two hours' work a week and an ecommerce site with low-margin physical products shipped out of a warehouse, I would choose the former.

## Design

Is the design off-the-shelf or custom? Does it look good? A free design or bad design is worth nothing, whereas a brilliant custom theme has resale value entirely separate from the blog. Many designers make reasonable cash selling good blog themes.

## Domain Factors

We talk about domains elsewhere, but specifically when looking at valuing a domain you just have to be aware of how domain sales have gone over the years to know what to look for. Domains *can* sell for millions, but usually do not.

First, a .com is better than any other extension, without exception. After the extension is the name itself, its snappiness, brandability, and pronounce-ability. Is it small, snappy, easy to say, and easy to recall? Smaller names are also more rare. I believe all the three-letter .coms are taken and most of the four-letter ones too. I was lucky to get my four-letter company name!

Many SEOs like to have the keyword in the domain, and the world's most expensive domains tend toward dictionary words such as poker.com, business.com, and sex.com. This is because these domains have a potential for type-in traffic and instant recall rather than having to do a great amount of promotion.

# Calculating a Blog's Value

Blog sale prices are impossible to predict accurately. Ask 10 different blog-gers to value the same site, and you will get 10 different answers. A blog's value depends entirely on the buyer. Valuations can be affected by all sorts of variables, from why and by whom it is being bought, to today's economic headlines, the parties' moods, and how drunk they are!

Blogs are worth what someone is willing to pay; that is all we can tell with certainty.

My approach is to look mainly at profit. A multiple of profits is a fair approach and easy to work out:

Annual Profits = 12× Monthly Repeatable Profit

For your own purposes you also can work out additional asset value for things like the design, subscribers, and any interesting technologies you would be gaining ownership of. If they are worth more than the asking price you might buy just to get access to them, or if the blog doesn't work out you might still recoup some money through sales:

**Assets = (Design Value + Subscriber Value + Technology Value)**

Is the blog worth a premium because of its content or traffic? Some blogs are bought on traffic alone, valuing each individual unique monthly visitor at so many cents to come to a total value:

**Premium = (Flagship Content Value + 12× Monthly Free Traffic Value)**

So for your own use you might bid up to a maximum of Profit + Assets + Premium. As I say, it is all subjective and you should never make a high first offer; consider this calculation as your maxium!

---

**PROBLOGGER BLOG TIP: LEARN THE MARKET**

In real-estate investing the advice is to learn your market. The same is true with virtual real estate, too. Where with houses you would get to know an area, type of property, and some of the people involved, with blog sales it is good to hang out at the popular blog sales sites and see what prices they go for, which sell, and which languish with zero bids. This helps you develop a "sixth sense" for blog valuations before you spend time looking at the numbers.

---

# Buying a Blog

Shop around and watch some auctions (see Figure 6-3) from the sidelines before diving in. Always remember if you are buying a blog that the listing details are not a replacement for due diligence! Never take the owners at their word. There is nothing there to enforce the truth on the part of the seller, so be extremely cautious and suspicious of anything claimed.

Find out as much as you can. Why are they selling? Do a background check on the seller using Google, Archive.org, and domain tools such as Whois .domaintools.com, and look to see if they are selling in multiple locations.

| Listings in Category: Established Sites For Sale | | Lowest Price ▼ Sort | blog | Search This Category | | |
|---|---|---|---|---|---|---|
| Listing Title | Seller | Created | ▼ Price | Ends | Views |
| Giant Forum - AdminFusion.com - 6.7k Members - Well Respected <br> Tremendous Opportunity to Own a Large Webmaster Forum | Lee_D | 12 Dec 07 14:00 | $13,000 | 1d 2h | 2,937 |
| WPCustomization.com - PR5 Wordpress Coding Service, average $600 / month <br> Established WordPress theming website, lots of clients, known for great service, HUGE POTENTIAL! | danz1328 | 16 Dec 07 18:06 | $4,500 | 6h 34m | 581 |
| My online store of my scripts with earnings <br> $800+ month earnings website | edpudol | 12 Dec 07 09:23 | $4,200 | 9d 22h | 692 |
| Established Men's Blog For Sale - Great Traffic, Revenue <br> $432.31 In It's First Month Of Existence - Great Traffic - 120 Rss Subscribers | onemansgoal | 15 Dec 07 21:15 | $3,500 | 1d 10h | 826 |
| Growing MS Zune Community $700+/Month Profit. Top Ranked in Google. <br> all you need is more review and contents to bring it next level. | searchfordeal | 10 Dec 07 14:15 | $3,500 | 5h 39m | 652 |
| BlogUpper.com for sale. <br> Well promoted pr5 website for sale. | snipergrunge | 9 Dec 07 12:10 | $3,000 | 3d 1h | 689 |
| SweetHacks Technology Blog For Sale - Well Established Website <br> PR3 Blog with over 800 Uniques Daily and $500+ Monthly Revenue | Xaasid | 13 Dec 07 18:06 | $2,500 | 7d 6h | 757 |
| Fast Growing PR4 Fashion and Celebrities Website <br> 25'000 uniques/month and $120/month in Ad Revenues | yannisa | 13 Dec 07 03:46 | $2,100 | 6d 15h | 560 |
| For Sale: 2 year old PR5 dot com blog <br> Earn $500 per month with an established blog | bobmeetsworld | Yesterday 10:57 | $1,550 | 6d 0h | 783 |
| Pet Community Site <br> Everything pet related commuty | noniman | 12 Dec 07 01:18 | $1,500 | 9d 14h | 700 |

**Figure 6-3:** An example list of auctions.

Don't get caught up in the excitement of an auction. The "winner" doesn't win anything; an auction is still a purchase, not a competition. Some auctions happen very fast, whereas others take their time. The only way to guarantee a purchase is to pay the "Buy It Now" (BIN) price, which, of course, potentially means paying a higher price.

Don't be afraid to contact the seller with questions. Do not be embarrassed or shy — there is no such thing as a stupid question where your money is concerned.

In general, it is believed that the first to mention a figure usually loses, but of course sellers are not going to low-ball their own price. It is possible they are willing to take less if offered.

Only raise your bids slowly and in small increments. A common beginner's mistake is to unnecessarily raise bids too high too fast.

When the sale goes through, ensure that everything has your name on it, everything is backed up, and that you have all logins, passwords, URLs, licenses, and so on, including the following:

- Domain transfer
- Business name

- Hosting
- Database, software licenses, and code
- Subscriptions
- Feedburner
- Newsletter subscribers

Never join an auction unless you have a plan. What will you do with it if you win? Have your top price in mind and don't go over it. Always be prepared to back out if things don't feel right.

---

**EXERCISE**

Find some blog-for-sale listings, and see which excite or interest you and which do not. Try to determine the aspects that draw or repel you. This is useful knowledge for when you come to take the plunge yourself.

---

# Selling Blogs

When you are selling your blog you need to get the highest fair price you can achieve while not giving away too much insider information, which could be used to just rip off your ideas. It is a delicate line to follow and is best informed by watching other successful blog sales.

In general, you want to be open, polite, and cooperative. Anything else will make buyers smell a rat. Any evasiveness will be taken as a danger signal and a risk which at best lowers your price and at worst ruins the sale entirely.

Maximize value ethically by giving the blog a makeover in every department, just like if you were putting your home up for sale.

Non-competes can be popular; a lot of buyers do not want to purchase your blog only to see you a week later try to poach back your audience. If a buyer demands a non-compete you might be able to use it in the negotiations, but just be sure of what you are signing on for. Be warned: These things can be specific and short-term or so vague you might find your blogging days are over!

When the price is significant, consider getting legal advice. A short book or some-guy-on-the-Internet is no replacement for a good lawyer.

If you do not like the idea of sales or negotiations, ask around on the blog forums for an experienced-broker recommendation. In many cases this can work out well for all parties.

## Where to Sell Your Blog

The popular ways to sell small to medium-size sites is through auction at SitePoint and Digital Point (Figure 6-4). These venues are popular and respected. Suprisingly eBay, while being the world's best-known auction marketplace, is a bad place to get a good price for a blog as a seller and is rife with dodgy deals.

Performancing.com has a free sales forum for smaller deals, as do many other popular blogs.

Direct, private deals are where the big money is made. Word-of-mouth networks allow sales to be made without the time pressure of an auction, but on the other hand, they can be protracted and complicated negotiations.

Contacting a potential buyer directly is always an option, as is getting an offer to buy out of the blue. If you want to sell and are open to casual offers, consider telling your friends and readers that your blog is on the market.

An option many people do not consider is to approach blog networks. Blog networks grow by acquisition mostly and might even want to hire you to maintain them.

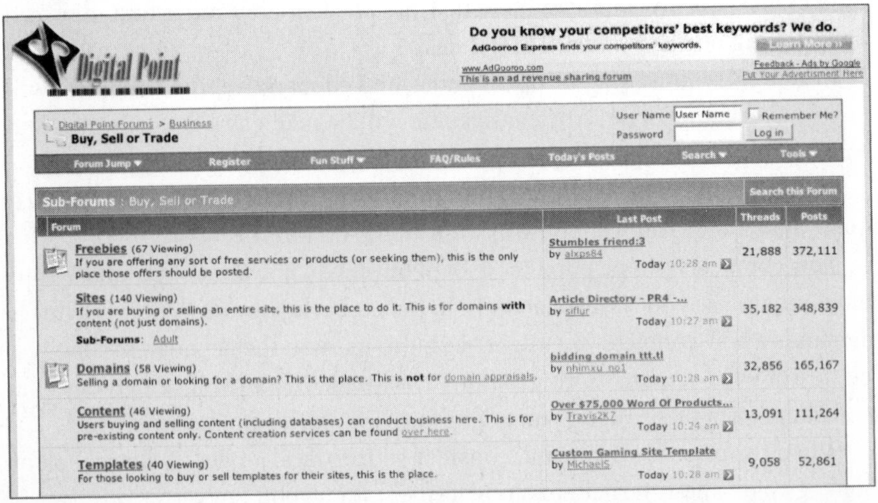

**Figure 6-4:** Digital Point marketplace.

**EXERCISE**

Imagine you have $50,000 to spend on buying a set of blogs. Go to the sites listed below and create a virtual portfolio. List the blog name and the price you would be willing to go up to. Revisit when the auctions are over to see how well your estimates compare. Would you be happy with your purchases?

```
http://forums.digitalpoint.com/forumdisplay.php?f=52
www.sitepoint.com/marketplace/
http://business.listings.ebay.com
http://flippa.com
```

## How to Sell Your Blog

Once you know you want to sell and have an idea how much you would accept, the next step is to do a listing. Some of the Blog Herald auction details are shown in Figure 6-5. The basic details you need to include in addition to any graphics are as follows:

- Blog name + URL
- Date started
- Description
- Hosting and software details
- Average monthly unique visitors, page views
- Inbound links according to Yahoo! and Google
- Monthly profits
- Posting frequency
- Auction end date
- Payment method
- Support offered

Determine a "Buy It Now" price to allow a buyer to end the auction with a purchase immediately. Something like a 4× annual profit multiple is not out of the question. You do not necessarily have to post a BIN right away. Starting bids are usually something like a 1× multiple.

## EXERCISE

Create a listing for your blog as if you are about to sell it. Can you put to hand all the necessary information? If you were to sell your blog now would any of your bullet points raise a red flag in the mind of a potential purchaser?

Like many online-community interactions, blog auctions attract the trolls and abusive idiots. Get ready to catch some heat as people use your listing for their own amusement and as an excuse to knock and insult from the safety of their anonymity.

**Blog Herald - Industry Leading Blog - 2K/Month - PR7**

**URL:** http://www.blogherald.com

**Age of site (months):** 36

**Monthly revenue:** 2000

**Revenue details:**
Typical monthly revenue streams:

Adzaar: $300
Adbrite: $100
Blogads: $250
Fastclick: $50
Google/ YPN; $400-600
Direct ads: average $100 per month
TextLinkAds: $200-300
Affiliate: 50-100$/month
Performancing: $325 gross (direct ad sale)
Other: $200-400

**Monthly page views:** 750000

**Traffic details:**
750K+ Pages/month
200K visitors/month
75K+ uniques/month

**Description:**
The Blog Herald is **the** industry leading blog news site. It has grown a reputation in the 3 years it has been serving the blog community as the place to go for blog-related news.

Typical readers include professional bloggers, journalists, analysts as well as regular bloggers who are just curious

**Figure 6-5:** Blog Herald auction details showing revenue and traffic.

## PROBLOGGER BLOG TIP: RAISE YOUR VALUE

Valuing a blog does not necessarily need to be performed only when you are ready to sell. It is a worthwhile habit to get into every few months. Seeing the growth in your blog value can be incredibly motivating! Is your blog growing in value? How can you improve the value of your blog? What aspects are holding you back and what do you need to work on?

## Summary

We have covered a lot of ground in this chapter and blog sales can be both exciting and nerve-rattling, but the basics are, in fact, simple sales. Just keep in mind that a blog is worth only what someone is willing to pay for it. Both the buyer and seller should keep that in mind; that way neither will feel cheated.

Income is the most reliable valuation method, but not every blog makes a profit, so other factors come into play and people are willing to buy blogs for more than just revenue alone.

Being successful at blog selling takes good sales and negotiation skills, but most of all if buying or selling, be careful and look out for potential scams.

# Blog Promotion and Marketing

**G**oing from zero to a decent-size audience is one of the hardest parts of blogging. Although some people seem to hit their stride effortlessly and instantly, getting an audience is something most of us have to work on.

Content is critical; it is the foundation of a good blog, but you still need more than that. Some people will tell you *all* you need is good content; unfortunately, reality is a little more complex, and I wouldn't suggest trying the "build it and they will come" formula. As I like to say, content might be king, but without posh clothes and an army to back him up, what is a king but an arrogant bloke in a funny shiny hat? Success in blogging means having great content backed by solid promotion — at least until your audience is big enough that your readers' word of mouth does the promotion for you.

A blog is not going to make you much money if nobody reads it. After writing content, promotion is probably the second most important activity of a blogger. This chapter takes you through how you can attract readers and, equally important, how to keep them.

## Building Readership

As I said in the introduction, content is critical. After all, that is what people will come to your blog looking for. There is daily, run-of-the-mill content; there is foundation or pillar content; and then there is *flagship content*.

# Building a Content Magnet

Anyone who has visited my chrisg.com blog and downloaded my free e-book is familiar with the term *flagship content*. Essentially, it goes above and beyond mere blog posts and works as a draw to your blog. It attracts people, because it provides a resource, a reference; something remarkable that is worth talking about.

When launching your blog, in addition to flagship "attraction" content, you need a good foundation of solid evergreen content. Darren calls this content "pillar" articles. A pillar article is usually a tutorial-style article that aims to teach your audience something useful. Generally, they are longer than 500 words and have lots of practical tips or advice. This evergreen type of article has long-term appeal, stays current (it isn't news- or time-dependent), and offers real value and insight. The more pillars you have on your blog, the better.

Do not rush this part; all the other traffic techniques depend on you having something useful to visit. If you think about it, what use is driving tons of visitors to something that is incomplete or not valuable?

While promoting, try to keep your blog fresh with useful posts. The important thing here is to demonstrate to first-time visitors that your blog is updated reasonably often, so they feel that if they come back they will likely find something new and worthwhile. If they think they have exhausted your blog's usefulness on the first visit, they will not bookmark or subscribe to it.

You don't have to produce one post per day all the time, but it is important that you do keep updating while your blog is brand-new. Once you get traction, you still need to keep the fresh content coming, but your loyal audience will be more forgiving if you slow down to a few posts per week instead. The first few months are critical, so the more content you can produce at this time the better.

## PROBLOGGER BLOG TIP: NOTICE POSTS YOU NOTICE

Half the battle of getting a blog off the ground is to have not just "good" content but *compelling* content. So, next time you stop to read an article, ask yourself why. What was it about this particular article that caught your eye? How had the author presented it? Analyze the headline, where you found it, and most importantly, how you can integrate these lessons into your own blogging.

# Blog Relations

Word of mouth is critical in promoting blogs. You need your blog to be memorable and spreadable. The first thing to sort out is your blog name. Use a proper domain name if you can, because the easier your URL is to remember, the more likely it will be recalled. Try to get a .com if you can because that is the most widely understood domain, and focus on small, easy-to-remember, catchy domains rather than fuss about having the correct keywords.

Consider some of the blogs you know and love — ProBlogger, CopyBlogger, BoingBoing (Figure 7-1), chrisg.com, and so on. These blogs have memorable names rather than being stuffed with search phrases like make-money-online-blogging.com.

**Figure 7-1:** www.boingboing.net

## Comment and Link Generously

As soon as you have five to ten pillar articles, start commenting on other blogs. You should aim to comment on blogs focused on a niche topic similar to yours because the readers there will more likely be interested in your blog.

Most blog commenting systems allow you to have your name linked to your blog when you leave a comment. This is how people find your blog. If you are a prolific commenter and always have something valuable to say, people will be interested in reading more of your work and hence click through to visit your blog. Do not place links in the comments unless they are highly relevant to the discussion. If in doubt, leave it out. This is not the time to be labeled as a spammer. Once you are better known, people may give you the benefit of the doubt, but as a newcomer, people will be highly suspicious of your motives.

Link generously and in context to other blogs in your posts. On some blogs, if you link to them they will link back automatically using "Trackbacks." What this does is leave a truncated summary of your blog post on their blog entry — it's sort of like your software telling someone else's blog that you wrote an article mentioning them. Trackbacks often appear like comments. Not all bloggers support Trackbacks due to the number of spammy Trackbacks being received.

Though linking out might not always earn you an automatic link back, it does often get the attention of the other bloggers. They will likely come and read your post, eager to see what you wrote about them. They may then become loyal readers of yours or at least monitor you. If you are lucky, some time down the road they may do a post linking to your blog, bringing in more new readers. Links from other bloggers are your very best source of new subscribers.

Encourage comments on your own blog as much as you can, especially in the early days when each comment is precious. One of the most powerful ways to convince someone to become a loyal reader is to show that there are other loyal readers already following your work. If they see people commenting intelligently and warmly on your blog, they infer that your content must be good because you have nice readers, so they should stick around and see what all the fuss is about. To encourage comments, simply pose a question in a blog post or ask friends to drop by and comment. But be sure to always respond to comments, to keep the conversation going.

---

**EXERCISE**

Do the blogs you frequent link often, or do they tend to hoard their audience? How often do you see familiar bloggers' names in blog comments? Make an effort to comment on a new blog every day and see if you notice any positive effects.

---

## Network and Communicate

Popular blogs often run projects and blog carnivals that can bring you some visibility. A blog carnival is a post in a blog that summarizes a collection of articles from many different blogs on a specific topic. The idea is to collect the best content on a topic in a given week. Often many other blogs link back to a carnival host, and as such, the people who have articles featured in the carnival often enjoy a spike in new readers.

Networking is critical, so join forums, email lists, and newsgroups within your niche. Don't comment just for the sake of it; try to add value to conversations. When readers reach out to you with a comment, email or link from their blog and follow up and interact with them. For starters, it's good manners, and it's also a good way to increase the chances that they'll return. Interact with those visitors who do try out your blog, and make it the best experience you can for them, and you'll find that they spread the word for you.

If you can make friends with fellow bloggers through commenting and participating in forums, you can ask for links. Do not be a pain; carefully consider the other bloggers' needs. Be smart, genuine, helpful, and polite. Rather than petitioning bloggers in a selfish way, put forward your link in a beneficial way that makes sense for them and their audience.

Add a signature to your outgoing email. This is an oldie, but a goodie. Many bloggers do this. Simply add the domain name to your outgoing email. Most email programs will allow you to do this automatically via a signature option. However, be careful with automatic signatures if you don't want your blog to be read by everyone that you email.

Promote subscription options to encourage first-time visitors to come back; put it in the sight of your readers by placing your RSS button in the most prominent position you can. There are a variety of different buttons that you can make available to readers to help them to subscribe to your blog via their news aggregators with one click that might also be worth investigating. Also provide the option to subscribe via email for those without RSS-reading accounts or software.

### EXERCISE

If you are not a member of a blogging community, now is the time to get involved. Blogging forums are a source of a great deal of support and technical advice and are also excellent places to network.

Darren runs a professional blogger community at `http://problogger` `.com` and Chris runs a free authority blogger community at `http://forum` `.authorityblogger.com`.

## Requesting Links from Bloggers

Emailing bloggers for links can work if you do it delicately and respectfully. Get it wrong and, at best, your email will be ignored.

Bloggers get hundreds of these types of emails; the more popular your blog is, the more of them you get. Sheer quantity and poor quality add up to such messages getting a poor reputation. Now I make it clear that I respond to very few, and I rarely reply to them.

Never, ever have a link request email as your first conversation with a blogger. Get to know them first. Do not be surprised, either, if a blogger that you think you know well ignores your link requests.

You have a much better chance of success if you follow this advice:

- **Be human** — Talk to bloggers as human beings; the more automated the email feels, the more likely it is to be deleted.
- **Be truthful** — Don't lie and say you have loved a site for a long time that you only just discovered. If you do actually like it, tell them why. Even better, tell them how you would improve it (without being insulting). I laugh every time people say they have been reading one of my brand-new blogs for years. Deceit, no matter how well intentioned, is a bad way to start a conversation.
- **Be specific** — The more vague you are, the more likely I am to not believe you. Do your research and stay away from generalities.
- **Be polite** — Demands do not wash. The other blogger does not owe you anything. All the cost is theirs, and the majority of the gain is yours. You are sending a humble request; make it read that way.
- **Be interesting** — You have to sell your proposition. People are not going to link to you just because you ask. There is a high probability your email will not be read past the first few lines, so make them count.
- **Be deserving** — Harsh but true. Would you write about something nobody will ever find interesting or useful just because someone begged you to? What about your article will the blogger and their audience find interesting, useful, valuable, or entertaining?

The key point is to be interesting. What about this proposition ought the other blogger find interesting? "Because I asked" doesn't work. Picture what you are giving the other blogger to work with. You need to have an interesting story to write about and be able to spell out how that is the case.

Would you approach a potential date you just met by saying, "Let's go back for coffee"? You wouldn't pitch a story to a newspaper or magazine editor with, "Please write about me; I already wrote about you," would you?

Keep it real, be specific, keep it brief without being rude, and state the hook, idea, angle, or benefit. I guarantee you will get a much better reaction.

> **EXERCISE**
>
> Check out the downloads in the Problogger Book Member Download Area for more tips on generating traffic:
>
> ```
> http://probloggerbook.com/bonus/
> ```
>
> If you have not already, sign up here: (Make sure you type the address exactly as shown.)
>
> ```
> http://probloggerbook.com/?/register/bonus.
> ```

Emailing link requests and guest posting are not the only way to get links, fortunately; a popular technique is to write a *link bait* post.

# Gaining Attention through "Link Baiting"

The term "link baiting" (also seen as one word, "linkbait") is used by webmasters to describe a variety of practices, all of which seek to generate incoming links to a website or blog from other sites.

It is actually a difficult term to be definitive about because it covers a lot of different practices, ranging from running awards or competitions, writing snarky attack posts on high-profile bloggers in the hope of them biting back and linking to you, through to providing other bloggers or site owners with useful tools.

In reality the term "link baiting" is a new term for something old. On the Web links are currency; therefore webmasters did all they could to get links from the earliest days of the Web.

## Is Link Baiting Ethical?

Link baiting is often written about in negative terms. I regularly see people writing off a post that others have written or a comment others have left as "just another link bait."

I personally don't like the term "link baiting," on some levels, because of these negative connotations. "Baiting" gives a sense of trying to trick or trap an unsuspecting person into doing something that they don't really want to do. Although this is accurate with some forms of link baiting, it is not true with others.

There is a lot of debate around both the term "link baiting" and some of the practices that people talk about it incorporating. Some argue strongly that it is just a by-product of quality content, others argue that many link-baiting strategies border on spam, and others seem to talk about link bait as being the answer to all Web promotional problems (increasingly SEO companies are offering link-baiting services).

My opinion on whether link baiting is good or bad is that it depends upon the type of link baiting that you're talking about. I think some techniques that people use are good standard blogging techniques, whereas other things that people do in the pursuit of links are destructive to the blogging community, and I'd argue against them.

Like almost anything online, people use link-baiting strategies for good and useful purposes but also for dubious and unethical ones. I guess in part we each need to think about our priorities, values, and even intentions as we go about our blogging and explore this topic.

## Successful Link-Bait Ideas

It is impossible to come up with a definitive list of what these practices are, because they are limited only by your imagination! In general, each tactic uses a "hook" or some type of novelty. Use the following list of ideas for inspiration:

- **Tools** — Create a useful, fun, newsworthy, or cool tool.
- **Quizzes** — Quizzes, surveys, and personality tests, such as, "Which Star Wars character are you?" have long been popular with web users.
- **Competitions** — Organize a contest or drawing with a valuable prize.
- **Scoops** — Be first with the news or to try something new.
- **Awards** — Create an award for your niche.
- **Lists** — List the 10 best blogs in your niche, or the top products, and so on. Look to glossy magazines for inspiration; they are full of lists! See Figure 7-2 to see how lists continue to work, despite some backlash.
- **Statistics** — Do a survey and release the results. One of my clients used to do a global survey relatively inexpensively that got them massive attention.

- **Freebies** — Give away something of value.
- **Interviews** — Interview a celebrity or someone popular in your niche.
- **Resources** — Create the ultimate resource or reference for a topic.

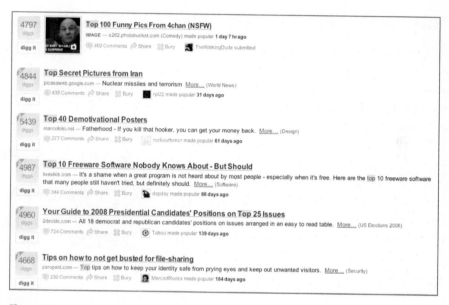

**Figure 7-2:** Lists continue to do well.

Why did I not list items that commonly appear in link-bait advice, such as "controversy" and "attack"? I have found that though you might garner some short-term attention, the long-term damage you would do to your reputation is simply not worth it.

The best link bait gathers links over time and grows with age. Next time you bookmark something, consider why you did so, and then use that knowledge to improve your next link bait.

Let's investigate one technique in depth: competitions.

**EXERCISE**

Scan through Digg, Reddit, and other social bookmarking sites, and note the headlines and introductions. Count how many "Top *X*" lists you can find. See if you can find ideas that would work in your niche. Which headlines beg to be clicked, and which leave you cold?

## Running Competitions

An increasing number of bloggers have been using competitions to create a buzz on their blogs. Figure 7.3 shows an example ProBlogger competition.

**Figure 7-3:** An example ProBlogger competition.

Two benefits of running competitions on your blog are:

- **New readers** — Competitions are potentially good for drawing new readers to your blog if you have a way to get the message out.
- **Reader stickiness** — Knowing there is a competition result to come prevents people from leaving; otherwise they will not see if they won.

The risks with competitions are:

- **Distraction from usual content** — Your regular visitors do not come to see competition content, so they might become disenfranchised.
- **Few winners, many losers** — You cannot supply a prize for every participant, so many people will be disappointed.

My own experience with competitions is that if you design your competition well, you can get the benefits without the downsides hurting too much. Here are some tips:

- **Build an audience** — Although competitions can generate traffic, you need to have a critical mass of readers before launching in order to build participation.
- **Identify goals** — Before you design your competition you need to work out why you're having it. What is your aim? How will you measure the competition's success? Once you have your goals you can then make better decisions about the competition format, prizes, promotion, and so on.
- **Offer prizes** — A number of thoughts come to mind when choosing prizes for a competition. Prizes should be:
  - **Relevant** — Match the prizes that you offer to your blog.
  - **Worthwhile** — The better your prizes are, the more buzz you will potentially create.
  - **Affordable** — Don't spend so much that you won't recoup the value.
- **Use sponsors** — One way to share the load with a competition is to have a sponsor for it. If you have a decent-size readership, you might be able to find a sponsor simply by asking.
- **Use affiliate links** — To help cover the cost of prizes, choose prizes that you can promote using affiliate programs.
- **Make requirements achievable for participants** — Don't make participants jump through too many hoops.
- **Make requirements achievable for you** — Competitions can be hard work, and people expect fair play. Don't make things more difficult than necessary.
- **Make just entering valuable** — An added incentive could be a free link to all participants, or just being something they get fun out of in addition to a chance at winning.
- **Set a reasonable competition length** — You don't want it to drag on for so long that your readers become sick of it, but on the other hand, you want it to be long enough for readers to enter, for the word to spread about it, and for sponsors to get their money's worth.

- **Promote your competition** — Unless you promote it, no one will know your competition is happening. Start your promotional efforts with your own readers via your blog, and also let your blogging friends know in advance. The best competitions have a mechanism for those participating to spread the word in some way; for example, if they refer a friend, they get additional entries in a draw.

# Search Engine Optimization for Blogs

The Web is full of great content that will never be seen outside of the author's screen. This is because the writer has failed to understand that just a few simple tweaks in the blogging process can increase search-engine visibility.

Many people try to paint search engine optimization as a nasty spammer tactic: "gaming" search-engine results for their own evil ends. This is simply not always the case. Like any powerful tool, it can be used for good or evil. Search engines are all about providing users the most relevant results. Good SEO helps that; bad fills the engine with spam.

People often ask me how to get ranked number one for a particular search result. Unfortunately, the only people with definitive answers work for the search engines themselves, and they are not talking. Darren and I read a lot of the best search people's advice on the topic, but virtually every article is a "best guess" of some kind.

The best advice for people wanting to optimize their blogs for search engines is to start with quality content on a specific topic and then tweak it using the current best practice.

Though SEO can seem complicated and mysterious and can become something of an obsession for blog owners, you should know that, more often than not, blogs are not quite well set up for SEO right off the bat.

Search engine optimization techniques fall into two broad categories: off-site and on-site techniques.

## Off-Site SEO

Off-site techniques are, as the name suggests, factors from outside the site that impact the blog's ranking in search engines. Many of these factors are outside the blogger's control; however, they are useful to know about. The most obvious and probably most powerful off-site factor is inbound links.

It is generally agreed that the links that point to a website are one of the most influential ways of climbing search-engine results. To put it most simply, every link to your site is seen by the search engines as being a vote of confidence in your site.

The best inbound links:

* Are from highly ranked sites.
* Are relevant to your topic.
* Use relevant and searched-for keywords.

Of course, you do not always have control over who links to you, but when you do have an influence over how you are linked, these are the types of links that you should be aiming for.

## How to Generate Quality Inbound Links

So how do you get such sought-after links? Now you know why we spent so much book space on discussing flagship content and link bait! Here are some more thoughts on how to attract quality links:

* **Offer valuable content** — The best way to get links to your blog is to write quality content that people will want to read. You can solicit links with others, sign up for different link-building programs, or even buy text links on other sites, but the cheapest and probably safest approach is to build inbound links in a natural, organic way, as others link to your quality content.
* **Notify relevant bloggers of your content** — Though I don't advocate spamming other bloggers and asking for links, I do recommend that if you write a quality post on a topic that you know will interest another blogger, it might be worth shooting them a short and polite email letting them know of your post (see the previous section on blogger relations).
* **Use directories** — An old way to generate inbound links was to submit your links to directories. I know of webmasters who still swear by the results of such a strategy, but I think the benefits are usually small at best.

- **Inter-link your blogs** — It is worth noting that you should be careful with this approach; if all your sites are hosted on one server, many think that search engines will work out what you're doing and the impact will be lessened.
- **Buy links** — Many professional webmasters have a budget to purchase links from other highly ranked and relevant sites. This is an expensive and high-risk strategy.
- **Swap links** — An older technique is to exchange links in a "you link to me and I will link to you" way. Be careful with this; the technique has a poor reputation due to spammers mass-mailing link-begging messages and other bad practices.

## On-Site SEO Techniques

On-site techniques are things that you do on your own blog that help build a higher ranking. As with all SEO techniques, there are many tactics and a lot of speculation around each of them.

Identify a few keywords for your article that you would like to be found in the search engines. What will visitors type into Google if they want information on the topic you're writing about? The answer to this question will give you a hint as to what words you'll want to see repeated throughout your article a number of times.

These keywords will need to be sprinkled throughout your article. You can feature keywords in the following ways with varying levels of influence on search results:

- In the URL
- Titles
- Links, in and out
- Bold text
- Heading tags (H1, H2, and so on)
- Image alt tags
- Throughout the text of your post, especially early on, in the first few sentences

Of course, if you go over the top with keywords it will ruin your article. Don't sacrifice your readers' experience of your site just for the sake of SEO.

Yes, keywords can be important in improving search-engine rankings, but more important is to ensure your content and design are user-friendly and helpful to readers. A site that is stuffed with keywords will appear spammy, so don't fall for the temptation.

Use internal linking to increase the visibility of other articles in your blog and use good keywords in the anchor text. Also make sure every page links back to your main page and any other important pages on your site. If you're writing on a topic you've previously written about, consider linking to what you've written before or use a "relevant posts" feature at the base of your article. You'll see that both Darren and I link key categories and articles from our sidebars and menus. One of the impacts of having them highlighted in this way is that because they are being linked from every page, they have become some of the most highly ranked articles.

In general you want each article to be focused on one topic. The more tightly focused the theme of a page, the better where search engines are concerned. Sometimes you might find yourself writing long posts that end up covering a number of different topics. They might relate loosely, but if search-engine ranking is what you're after it could be better to break up your post into smaller, more focused pieces.

Avoid duplicate content as much as possible. Google warns publishers in its guidelines about having the same content on more than one page. This goes for both multiple pages that you own and also pages outside your site. This is because a tactic of spammers is often to reproduce content on many pages or to steal content from other sites. There is some debate over what duplicate content does and doesn't include, but the best advice is to be very careful about how many places your content appears.

Use the Google Webmaster Tools (Figure 7-4) to check if there are any problems that are causing your site not to be indexed properly. You can also see the phrases for which you are currently ranked. The website is `http://www.google.com/webmasters/`.

**EXERCISE**

Put some searches into Google for phrases that apply to your niche. Who comes out on top? Take a look at the pages listed in the results. Can you work out why they rank higher than the rest?

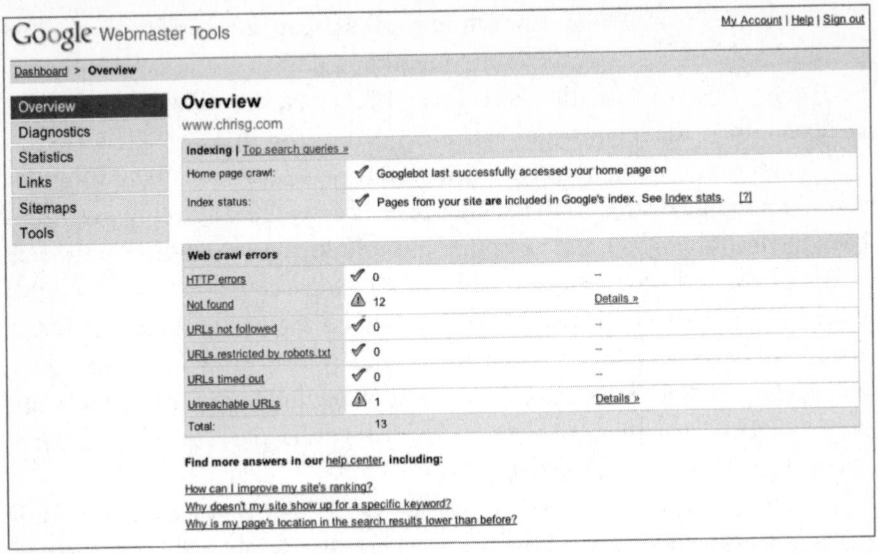

**Figure 7-4:** Google's Webmaster Tools.

# Increase Page Views on Your Blog

As well as getting new visitors, it is important to keep visitors interested. Keeping your readers engaged and coming back is just as important as finding new ones.

Statistics have revealed that the average blog reader views around one and a half pages every time they visit a blog. The more pages a typical visitor reads, the better the job you are doing. What can we do to get readers to view more pages? Let's explore a few possibilities:

- **Highlight related posts** — One of the more common practices of bloggers to encourage readers to read multiple pages on their blogs is to highlight related posts at the end of your article.
- **Interlink within posts** — A similar but perhaps more effective technique is to highlight relevant posts within the content of your posts. If you're writing a post that mentions something similar to what you've written before, simply link to your previous post from within your article.

For example, I've written about this technique previously in a post on increasing the longevity of key posts.

- **Highlight key posts and categories in your sidebar** — Highlighting your category pages is another useful technique to encourage your readers to find more posts on the same topic. To explicitly name what your category is can also be useful. That is, rather than just having the category name at the end of the post, try something like "read more posts like this in our XYZ category."

- **Create compilation pages** — Darren has a page at ProBlogger that lists his top 20 posts, and we have a "best of" list at Performancing.com also. Many first-time readers use these pages to discover content to read. Every post a visitor reads increases the chances that they will become loyal readers.

- **Write a series** — You need to be careful with writing series of posts over periods of time, but they are a great way to keep readers coming back, and once they are complete to have them surf through multiple pages on your blog. Don't create series just for the sake of increasing page views, of course — this can really frustrate readers — but use them on longer posts or when you genuinely want to cover a larger topic over time.

- **Use excerpts** — There is always debate over this topic. Should you show the full article on your homepage and feed or snippets? If you only have partial content visible, the reader *has* to click through to see the full thing. Though this is certainly a benefit of partial feeds, doing so will cause some readers to unsubscribe to your blog completely. This is a cost/benefit scenario that individual bloggers need to weigh.

- **Be interactive** — An effective way to get readers coming back to your blog many times over a day is to have a blog that people want to interact with. Liz Strauss has "open mike" events in her comment area at Successful-blog.com and this has made the blog less of a publication and more of a party!

## Build Community and Get More Comments

Jakob Nielsen's usability study found that 90 percent of online-community users are lurkers (read or observe without contributing), with only 9 percent of users contributing "a little" and 1 percent actively contributing.

So 1 percent of your blog's users are actively engaging with your blog, and the rest are at best occasional contributors.

The study isn't just on blogging, so the actual numbers could be more or less than these and would no doubt vary from site to site anyway, but the principle holds true. The vast majority of readers leave a blog without leaving a comment or contributing to it in any way.

To some extent this is just the way it is, and we probably need to just get used to it; however, when it comes to comments there are some ways to encourage more interactivity on your blog:

- **Invite comments** — Regular readers of my blog will see I often invite people to comment, with a phrase such as, "What do you think? Please share your thoughts in the comments." When I specifically invite comments, people leave them in higher numbers than when I don't. Keep in mind that new readers that are unfamiliar with blogging don't always know about comments or how to use them, and sometimes people almost need to be given permission.

- **Ask questions** — Including specific questions in posts definitely helps get higher numbers of comments. I find that when I include questions in my headings, it is a particularly effective way of getting a response from readers because you set a question in their mind from the first moments of your post.

- **Be incomplete** — If you say everything there is to say on a topic, you're less likely to get others adding their opinions, because you'll have covered what they might have added. Though you don't want to purposely leave too many things unsaid, there is an art to writing open-ended posts that leave room for your readers to be experts also.

- **Be interactive** — If you're not willing to use your own comments section, why would your readers? If someone leaves a comment, then reply. This gets harder as your blog grows, but it's particularly important in the early days of your blog because it shows your readers that their comments are valued, it creates a culture of interactivity, and it gives the impression to other readers that your comments section is an active place that you as the blogger value. As the activity in your comments section grows, you may find you need to be slightly less active in it because readers will start to take over on answering questions and creating community; however, don't completely ignore your comment threads.

- **Be humble** — I find that readers respond very well to posts that show your own weaknesses, failings, and the gaps in your own knowledge rather than those posts where you come across as knowing everything there is to know on a topic. People are attracted to humility and are more likely to respond to it than to a post written in a tone of someone who might harshly respond to their comments.

- **Be gracious** — Related to humility is grace. There are times where you as the blogger will get something wrong in your posts. It might be spelling or grammar; it could be the crux of your argument or some other aspect of your blogging. When someone leaves a comment that shows your failing it's very easy to respond harshly in a defensive manner. We've all seen the flaming that can ensue. Though it's not easy, a graceful approach to comments, where you admit where you are wrong, can bring out the lurkers and make them feel a little safer in leaving comments.

- **Reward comments** — There are many ways of acknowledging and "rewarding" good comments that range from "reader appreciation" posts through to highlighting particularly good comments in other posts that you write. Drawing attention to your readers who use comments well affirms them and also draws the attention of other readers to make good use of your comments section.

- **Make it easy to comment** — I leave a lot of comments on a lot of blogs each week, but there is one situation where I rarely leave a comment even if the post deserves it — blogs that require me to log in before making a comment. Maybe I'm lazy (actually — there's no maybe about it!), or maybe there's something inside me that worries about giving out my personal details, but when I see a comments section that requires registration I almost always (95 percent or more of the time) leave the blog without leaving the comment that I want to make. Though I totally understand the temptation to require registration for comments (combating spam in most cases) something inside me resists participating in such comments sections. Registration is a hurdle you put in front of your readers that some will be willing to leap but that others will balk at (the same is often said about other comments-section requirements that go beyond the basics). Keep your comments section as simple and as easy to use as possible.

PROBLOGGER BLOG TIP: IT'S ALL IN THE ENGAGEMENT

Page views are a consequence of reader engagement. How interested you keep your visitors over a period of time will translate into repeat visits and increased page views. What factors keep you returning to a particular blog? When have you found yourself reading page after page and when have you taken one look and never returned?

## Summary

Gaining and keeping readers comes down to having brilliant content and letting people know about it. This is a big job and should not be underestimated. Thankfully, although it is especially tough at the start, it gets easier as you build momentum.

# 8  Social Media and Your Blog

You cannot have missed the growing buzz around "social media" over recent years. It seems the television and newspaper media is obsessed with Twitter this and Facebook that. Perhaps this fixation is because the traditional media fear the new media as competition?

At its most general, social media encompasses every sort of social or community site, but each service or tool can be broadly categorized as "Social Bookmarking," "Media Sharing," and "Social Networking."

This chapter shows you how you can use these various social media tools to your advantage.

## Determining Which Social Media Sites to Use

Deciding which social media site to use depends largely on your goals and where your audience hangs out. Your most desired outcome determines which tools to use and how you interact with them. Social media services can deliver terrific benefits to you and your blog, and they are especially good for attracting attention, and for engagement. With attention you will potentially grow your links and subscribers, and with more engagement you will deepen networking connections and retain more loyalty.

The confusion arises when trying to make distinctions, because all of these sites are blending features, with all social media sites allowing you to add friends, and most sites encouraging you to share or rate content.

In terms of promotion, the main draws are social bookmarking sites such as Digg.com, StumbleUpon, and del.icio.us, and the high traffic media sharing sites, in particular YouTube. For networking you would look to Twitter, Facebook, and for business networking or job-seeking, LinkedIn.

## Social Bookmarking

You know when you find a useful site that you expect to need in future, you bookmark the site in your browser so you have an easy way to refer to it. Social Bookmarking started out as a way to share your bookmarks, so rather than sitting on your computer you have them wherever you go and your friends can access them too. The most famous of these sites is probably Delicious.com but Delicious has waned in popularity and fame, in favor of the new breed lead by Digg.com.

Each of these sites has the potential to send you thousands of visitors, and they all work by members submitting content and allowing others to judge it or vote for it in some way. Getting popular on these services has turned into an obsession for many bloggers, which can be dangerous when it distracts you from looking after your regular readers.

## Social Networking

On the other side are the Social Networking sites, which are all about creating connections between people and fostering communication.

In general, the features you expect to see on a Social Networking site or service are the ability to create a profile about yourself, add people who you know or discover to a list of friends, and to send messages to your contacts. Some services started out as glorified "address books," but once the members started interacting, the appeal quickly turned to having discussions and sharing links and content.

## Media Sharing Services

This type of social media service blends many of the features of the other two.

Media sharing services started out as a way to store and share your own content, such as uploading your pictures to online photograph albums so that your family overseas can see your wedding images.

Just like social networking sites you can befriend other users, and also much like social bookmarking sites there is often a way to rate or comment on content that other people share.

Every type of digital media has a popular service supporting it, from video through to PowerPoint presentations, if you have content there will be a place to share it.

# Implementing Social Media Promotion

Social networking sites can drive traffic, and some of the media sharing sites have terrific traffic potential, but for promotion, the biggest traffic *spikes* come from the social bookmarking services, so we look at those first.

To get traffic from a social bookmarking site your article must be submitted and get a lot of votes. This works differently for each service. Traffic from StumbleUpon comes via a special toolbar that you can download from its site. On the others you have to log in, find the appropriate article, and then hit the bookmark or vote button.

Because there are so many services it is best to focus on just a few. I mainly focus on StumbleUpon because with just a few votes you can get a nice flow of traffic. I have friends who focus on Digg because, although it is far harder to get visible, when your content gets to the front page you get a huge traffic spike. Figure 8-1 shows an example of a traffic graph from one of my blogs.

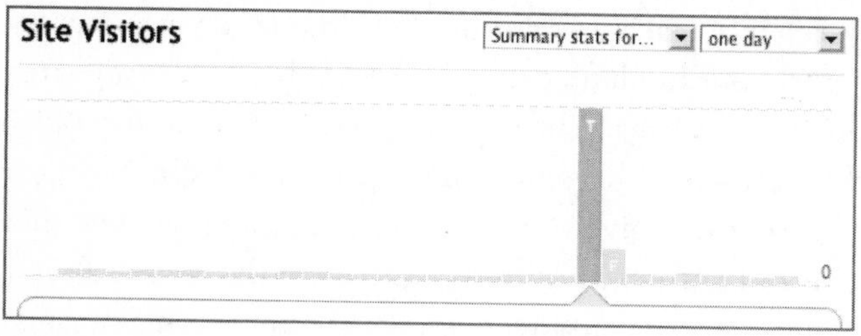

**Site Visitors**     Summary stats for... ▼   one day ▼

**Figure 8-1:** An example graph showing a traffic spike.

# Writing for Social Bookmarking Success

In general, social media users are surfing. They are not keen on investing much time to discover if something is worthy of attention, so you have to pull out all the stops featured in Chapter 4:

- Write attention-grabbing headlines.
- Keep your paragraphs short and punchy.

- Use bullets, images, and subheads to aid skimming.
- Pull out interesting quotes and key points.
- Make it something people will want to talk about, share, or come back to.

## Social Bookmarking as a Popularity Contest

You will find the content that does well in social bookmarking sites in general is very similar to the kind of content that bloggers are inclined to link to, so the tried and tested link-bait tactics shown in Chapter 7 work well. Just take care to monitor the target service to see what tends to be popular and what attracts few votes. Also make lots of friends; you will need their votes to get your content seen.

Most of these bookmarking sites allow you to send a link to your friends for their voting consideration. In addition you can put buttons on the article itself, and, of course, email your friends to get them to vote for it.

Becoming successful with social media is a lot like high school, really. Being "nice" is great, but being popular and having lots of friends is far more important. Obviously the quantity of friends is not the only criteria; there is no point in having 10,000 fans that ignore you, so you need a quantity of *engaged* contacts to make any kind of headway.

To even get a story seen in social bookmarking sites, you need votes. Hardly anyone looks in the dark and hidden corners of social bookmarking sites where new and unnoticed stories live. The popular pages get all the attention, followed by pages that are about to become popular with a little push.

You need a bunch of friends to give you a kick start. You can see how this works on StumbleUpon in Figure 8-2. Although the more the better, do not spam people, or you will suffer the consequences, which range from not gaining any benefits because your stories are automatically buried so your content is effectively invisible, through to at worst being banned.

Having some friends who are already popular will help you; if you hang out with the cool crowd, your stuff gets far more attention. This is because sites, such as Digg, rank users based on usage history. If they have a pattern of supporting successful articles, their votes gain more weight.

**Figure 8-2:** StumbleUpon's share feature.

Friends and adoring fans can help you get your stuff noticed. Most of the work, then, is done for you. In fact, that can be all that is required. Sometimes, however, people see your content and "bury" it; yes, you can also get voted down.

You shouldn't be at all surprised when that happens if your article doesn't have any substance. Unfortunately, just like high school, there is a ruling-class clique with their own likes, dislikes, and prejudices. Being popular is not enough if you break the unwritten rules. Being unwritten they can change without notice and I can not list them here, but each community has developed a character and bias which becomes obvious from observing the popular content and comment areas. When you are using social media, hang out and observe. Look at what gets popular, what stays popular long-term, and what gets to the front page and then disappears just as fast.

---

---

Most people will tell you what works on Digg traditionally had to have some relationship with more geeky topics. Though this is still somewhat true, the demographics are changing to include more of the general population. Articles featuring Apple, Linux, Xbox, and so on still make a strong showing. Duplicated information and overly commercial, or overly self-promotional content do not do as well.

Unlike the way it was in high school, the young male geeks rule the roost. The same old advice applies here as much as anywhere else: Consider your audience. What will they enjoy and get value from? What is the best way to deliver it? What do you need to do to appeal to them?

## Driving Traffic with YouTube

YouTube is the dominant video sharing service where you can find video clips about everything from people falling over through to the latest music promos. If some instant is on video, you can be sure someone has shared it on YouTube, legally or otherwise.

Thanks to YouTube's huge popularity and its near monopoly, YouTube videos can attract a tremendous amount attention. Figure 8-3 gives one example of this high visibility: Just one version of the Susan Boyle *Britain's Got Talent* audition video at the time of writing has received over 82 million views and over 368,000 ratings! To put that into perspective, the actual television show the clip was recorded from was considered a hit with over 12 million viewers at broadcast.

YouTube became such a dominant force that Google decided to stop trying to compete with it and bought it. Now YouTube is considered, by traffic, to be the Internet's second biggest search engine!

**Figure 8-3:** Susan Boyle video.

People search YouTube itself, but Google also gives YouTube content prominent placement in its search results. As you can see in Figure 8-4, Google
places the Google News and YouTube results *above* the official Susan Boyle
website.

This means if you create a popular video with the name and description
matching a sought after search term you are likely to attract a good portion
of that traffic.

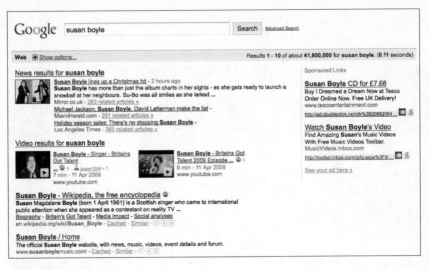

**Figure 8-4:** Google search results for Susan Boyle.

Another way to get more traffic through YouTube is to post your own video as a response to a popular video, as shown in Figure 8-5 or have it appear as a related video, as shown in Figure 8-6. People checking out your video after they view the original video drive up your traffic.

**Figure 8-5:** Posting a video response drives up your traffic.

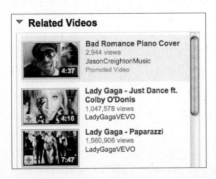

**Figure 8-6:** You can post a video as related to grab some of the traffic a popular video is already attracting.

**PROBLOGGER BLOG TIP: CREATE VIDEO EASILY**

When most people think about creating video they worry about needing technical expertise and expensive equipment, but in fact a YouTube video could easily be created with Camtasia or other screen recording software, a cheap cell phone or Flip style camera. Content is the important part, do not let lack of Hollywood polish hold you back from creating.

Of course so far all this traffic is taking place on YouTube and not benefiting your blog, so if you want to attract free traffic instead of spending money on YouTube advertising, you have to make sure your video contains your blog web address. Include it as a caption, water mark, or some kind of logo. Be sure to place the link to your blog early in the description so it does not get cut off after the more info link.

**EXERCISE**

Search YouTube for videos from your niche and create a response video adding your own take. Try to contribute some valuable tips or opinions of your own while acknowledging the original video.

# Engaging Your Followers with Social Media

Social media is not just about generating traffic and getting attention. It can also be a key way to keep your audience interested and loyal, build your brand, and generate more networking opportunities.

Many people now look to Twitter and Facebook as not just places where to keep track of the latest activities of friends, but also as a replacement for the traditional blog news feed. I am an example of this. At my peak I subscribed to over 800 feeds in Google Reader, but now I check in on feeds only occasionally and rely on Twitter to deliver scoops within in the niches I monitor.

No doubt many of your readers will be using these social tools in a similar way, so having a presence and grabbing your brand names as a Twitter account and Facebook vanity URL is worthwhile.

In addition to sharing your latest headline, you need to interact with people and treat them as human beings rather than just a source of clicks. This means having conversations and sharing cool content no matter who created it, not just your own.

## Using Twitter

Twitter was originally a service that allowed you to provide "Status Updates" in the form of answering the question "What are you doing." But while that was what it was intended for, it is now used in the following ways:

- Chatting
- Getting help and answers
- Sharing links
- Getting news updates
- Making friends and networking
- Marketing
- Sending and receiving reminders
- Getting automated alerts
- Worshiping celebrities

Essentially it has become a combination of news feed, gossip hub, and catch-all text messaging system.

My own relationship with Twitter has mutated over time. At first I didn't get it, I thought it was a narcissistic waste of time. Then I gave it another chance, and fell in love with it, but more importantly found it very useful.

Twitter is available from its website, Twitter.com, via desktop software services that work with the system, and through a mobile web version for smart cell phones. You can connect your email address, add your cell/mobile telephone number, and get text messages through the system.

The most popular Twitter client is currently TweetDeck.com which is available for Windows and Mac desktop, and also the iPhone.

## About Twitter Messages ("Tweets")

Twitter messages are limited to 140 characters (a "character" is a press of the keyboard key, a letter of the alphabet, space, number, and so on). This keeps Twitter messages down to a size compatible with mobile networks.

You might think this size constraint is a bad thing, but it is part of the appeal once you get used to it. Rather than pages of long, dreary monologues, you get a stream of snappy quips and informative nuggets. This short message style has lead to using the system being described as "Micro-blogging."

While competitors allow you to share images and other media, with Twitter, messages are plain text, but you can share links just by typing them out in full.

Long web addresses are automatically put through a web address shrinker, which conserves message space, but does lead to you not having a clue where you will be taken to if you click. If you are going to share a link, make sure you provide some context!

The service is still developing; both technologically (it is often down or unreliable) and in the way people use it.

### THE THREE GREAT NON-SOCIAL USES FOR TWITTER

Twitter is not just for chatting with friends. There are also real benefits for probloggers and businesses:

- **Inside scoop** — Follow the right industry insiders and you get the news before any other channel. I have gained access to information and beta accounts this way, and it can be very useful.
- **Traffic** — Drop a link with a good intro and you can see click-throughs and comments as a result. Track how many people clicked a certain link using a service such as Bit.ly, which as well as shrinking the web address down to a more manageable size, also counts clicks, and who shared the link. You get even more traffic and followers by being "Retweeted" where other people share the message you posted, so encourage other people to share your links by retweeting theirs!
- **Networking** — I have stated many times how important networking is for bloggers. Twitter is a growing venue for this with fewer barriers and gatekeepers. Make sure you link to your Twitter account from your blog and from your email signature to encourage people to follow you.

If you want more information about Twitter, check out Darren's Twitter blog, twitip.com.

### PROBLOGGER BLOG TIP: USE TWEETMEME TO GET MORE TRAFFIC

Twitter users are always looking for cool content to share, so help them share your great stuff by using the TweetMeme.com button on your blog. You can get copy and paste code or use the WordPress plugin. This adds a button to your articles that counts how many times the post has been retweeted and allows the visitor to click and retweet to their followers. Instant viral traffic opportunity!

**EXERCISE**

The best way to understand social networking is to get involved! Join the main social bookmarking sites and make some friends. Follow Chris and Darren on Twitter:

```
http://twitter.com/chrisgarrett
http://twitter.com/problogger
```

**FACEBOOK**

While Facebook started out as a very youthful environment, the demographic has widened now to include pretty much anyone. In fact, with a quoted 350 million users, with 35 million people logging in each day, Facebook now has a daily user base that dwarfs the population of many entire *countries*.

Much like a blog, Facebook allows you to update your account with notes, video, photographs and links, plus like Twitter you can post short "status updates" to tell your friends what you are up to.

In addition to normal user profiles, anyone with a business or a huge fan base can also create Facebook Fan Pages. With a normal user account you are limited to 5,000 friends, but with Facebook Fan Pages there is no limit to the number of contacts you can gather to a page.

Kick off your Facebook following by linking from your blog and from other social media accounts such as your tweets.

The key to Facebook success is to share cool stuff and to encourage friends to share your stuff with their friends to get a viral effect going.

**PROBLOGGER BLOG TIP: OBSERVE AND GROW YOUR SOCIAL MEDIA ENGAGEMENT**

Audience engagement is vital in social media just as it is with your blog. Having dozens of friends and fans is nice, but you need them to care about what you have to say in order to gain the real benefits. The first step is to "listen." Observe how your favorite social media users behave to get ideas for what works to increase and maintain social media engagement with your contacts.

## Summary

Social media can be fun and deliver enormous benefits to you and your blog, from increased traffic through to greater opportunities and income, but if you are not careful it can soak up a great deal of your time, killing your productivity, especially if you get absorbed in Facebook and Twitter chit-chat or watching hour after hour of funny YouTube videos. If you work social media into your blogging schedule consciously though, and learn what works for you, your blog and social media accounts can compliment and expand each other in fantastic and unexpected ways.

# Secrets of Successful Blogs

If you have read this far, it is safe to assume you would like to be successful in your blogging. As well as reading and researching as much as you can about the techniques and tactics involved in creating a popular and profitable blog, a great way to do well in any endeavor is to learn from the best examples.

You have an advantage today that the pioneers did not. The bloggers who have come before you have made many of the mistakes and learned what works, saving you the trouble! This chapter takes a look at some example blogs and bloggers to see how they have achieved success in blogging in their own ways.

## About Success in Blogging

What do we mean by "success"? For each blogger it will be something different. It could be fame, income, sales, size of audience, and so on. Even though Darren and I consider ourselves professional bloggers, we both arrived at it through our own routes and tactics. We earn money in different ways and have different goals. When you look at the other bloggers in this chapter, you can see how diverse professional blogging really is.

Before embarking on a blogging project, it is worth discovering what success would mean to *you*.

**EXERCISE**

Do you have a clear idea about what you want to achieve with your blogging? Take a moment to analyze your motivations; knowing what you hope to get out of blogging will help you focus your efforts on the things that will make it happen.

# Analysis of Top Blogs

When we looked at the top blogs and bloggers around us, we found there were certain elements in common between them, regardless of niche, monetization method, and motivation. In particular, age, posting frequency and social media all seem to focus heavily in their success.

## Blog Age

Darren did some research a while back and discovered that the average age of the most successful blogs was 33.8 months. The first lesson to take away is that blogging is a long-term thing, but it is possible to have success much faster with luck and a lot of hard work.

## Posting Frequency

In most analyses of top blogs, a noted trend is that the most successful bloggers post more than the rest. Usually they post many short posts a day. There seems a definite correlation between success and posting frequency.

It does make sense; the more posts you publish, the more chance for links and for readers to notice you. Search engines also like to see lots of fresh content, feeding as they do on text.

This can cause dismay for bloggers who struggle to keep pace. What you have to keep in mind is that most of the top blogs are written by multiple authors. Team blogs can easily keep up a high post rate, and often need to if they are in rapidly changing news niches, such as TechCrunch.com.

Lately, though, there has been a backlash against too high a posting frequency, with bloggers and readers both expressing a preference for fewer, better-written and well-thought-out articles. In many surveys on the question of why readers unsubscribe, "posting too often" usually ranks high.

**EXERCISE**

How often do your favorite blogs update? Are any of them updating a little too often? Do you find yourself skipping or missing posts? Do you look forward to the next post from a certain blog?

## Social Media Factor

Glen from Clickalite.com worked out that the Top 100 blogs achieved front-page stories on Digg.com 8,000 times between them. Most surprising was that the top five blogs did so 3,600 times between them — 45 percent of the total for the whole list.

Clearly the top blogs do well in social media. It's impossible without further analysis to know if this is correlation or causation, but it is an interesting statistic nevertheless.

Personally, I think it works both ways; Digg and other social media sites' popularity is both a contributor and a consequence of blog success and is a tactic I encourage in all the blogs for which I write.

## Revenue

The vast majority of successful blogs show advertising, with less than a quarter using Google AdSense.

It is worth noting that when blogs get to this sort of scale, they have the traffic and audience to demand excellent deals, even from Google.

Many of the top blogs now hire ad salespeople, use the services of specialist ad companies such as Federated Media, or are part of blog networks. At a certain size, a blog becomes a business by any definition, so they tend to work that way, with chief executives, editors, and writers.

## Blog Language

You might expect English to dominate blogging overall, but in terms of volume, Japanese takes the top spot with 37 percent, and English is second with 36 percent. When it comes to the Top 100, though, 80 percent are written in English.

PROBLOGGER BLOG TIP: NON-ENGLISH GROWTH

Expect to see a lot of growth of non-English blogs in coming years. Blogging is becoming increasingly popular around the world. If you can afford it or can find a linguist partner, it would be well worth having your articles translated.

# Learning from Niche Blogs

We have already recommended in this book that you at least start out blogging in a niche. The bloggers in this section have made their blogs so highly focused and so identified with their topic that they are the leaders and standard-bearers for their chosen topic.

- **Strobist.com** — A photography blog that, rather than focus on the whole topic of photography, went super-niche and wrote about using small, inexpensive flashes. Now David Hobby has been able to take a leave of absence from his job as a photo journalist and is earning money through running workshops and developing his own range of training products.

- **CopyBlogger.com** — Lots of bloggers write about blogging; Brian Clark decided to start a blog about the art and techniques of writing. Initially writing on his own and then bringing on guest writers (Chris included), CopyBlogger is now the most-popular blog on the subject and has been used as a platform to launch Brian's Teaching Sells online course.

- **Lifehacker.com** — Productivity is a massive subject online, and Lifehacker is probably the best known. Rather than just write about productivity in general, Lifehacker approaches the subject with a techie slant, which the audience really enjoys.

- **TheBudgetFashionista.com** — Many bloggers have written about fashion. Kathryn Finney took the niche and decided to write a blog for real women on real incomes, in a warm and friendly style. It has really worked; the blog is successful, has spawned a spin-off book, and has put Kathryn in the spotlight, with media and TV appearances on NBC, CNN, and Fox.

---

**PROBLOGGER BLOG TIP: SPOT AND ANALYZE SUCCESS**

Watching out for the lessons that are all around you is a great habit to get into. You can learn from the success of others in some surprising ways. It is not just about looking at fellow bloggers — read biographies or analyze your favorite celebrity or television show. Knowing how people got where they are helps you develop a success mindset.

## Lessons from Niche Bloggers

1. **Identify an underserved niche** — It is very difficult to get a photography blog noticed in today's blogosphere. David Hobby chose a micro-niche, a niche of a niche, and served it comprehensively with his Strobist blog. Make it easy on yourself, and choose a niche where you can make a difference.

2. **Define your blog's mission and articulate it in a benefits-led way** — If a reader sees your blog's mission and thinks "so what?" you have failed. Be sure your blog's mission helps the reader.

3. **Own your mission and stay focused** — It would be so easy for any of these blogs to see their growing audience as permission to cover anything they like. Once in a while they can get away with it, kind of like a pop star deciding to release a swing album. Too much, though, and the valuable and unique quality that attracted readers could go away.

---

**EXERCISE**

Out of all the blogs you know of, which would you categorize as niche and which would have more general appeal? Do these blogs change approach depending on their category?

---

# Learning from Top Blogs

Although it can be interesting looking at the Top 100 blogs as a whole, or categories of blogs, there are actually few similarities between them once you get past the factors detailed previously. To learn more, we need to look at some blogs individually.

## ProBlogger

It's only appropriate to start with ProBlogger, seeing as pro blogging is what this book is all about!

We have already covered the history of Darren's blog in this book, so no need to repeat it here. Suffice to say that ProBlogger is the blog people think of when they think about making money from blogging.

How did Darren make his blog the first choice among bloggers?

### Lessons from ProBlogger

1. **Be first** — There was a time when it was easy to have first-mover advantage. Of course, that was when hardly anyone had the foresight to start anything other than a personal diary blog. There are thousands of blogs now on every subject; how can you be first? Be different. Find a gap and fill it. Demonstrate the benefit of your unique take.

2. **Staying power** — It is tempting to hear of six-figure incomes and become despondent at your own meager Google check. Darren didn't get there overnight either. Some of my biggest mistakes in blogging have been quitting, chopping, and changing. Don't make my mistakes; learn from Darren. Stick with it!

3. **Show off your best stuff** — Put your popular stuff right up front where people can see it. When you visit this blog, you are not lost for things to read. After people read your post, do your readers know where they can go next?

4. **Community counts** — Great content is important, but when it is combined with a vibrant community, that is when your blog will really take off.

5. **Test and research** — Blogging is a moving target. Working out what works and which tactics do not takes research, experimentation, testing, and discussion. Over the years, Darren experimented with new developments from MyBlogLog.com to Chitika.com. Make sure you keep up with the times.

6. **Privacy** — Don't reveal too much personal information. Decide what you are going to keep private, and make it stay that way.

7. **Stay positive** — I don't think I have ever seen Darren go off on a rant. This builds up a tremendous amount of goodwill. You will never hear a bad word said about him. Blogging success is as much about networking as it is good writing. What are people thinking and saying about you?

# TechCrunch

TechCrunch (Figure 9-1) is the most popular tech news site. Mike Arrington has taken the blog from nowhere to being the site that can make or break tech startups. He employs a staff of writers spread around the globe, so there is almost 24-hour coverage.

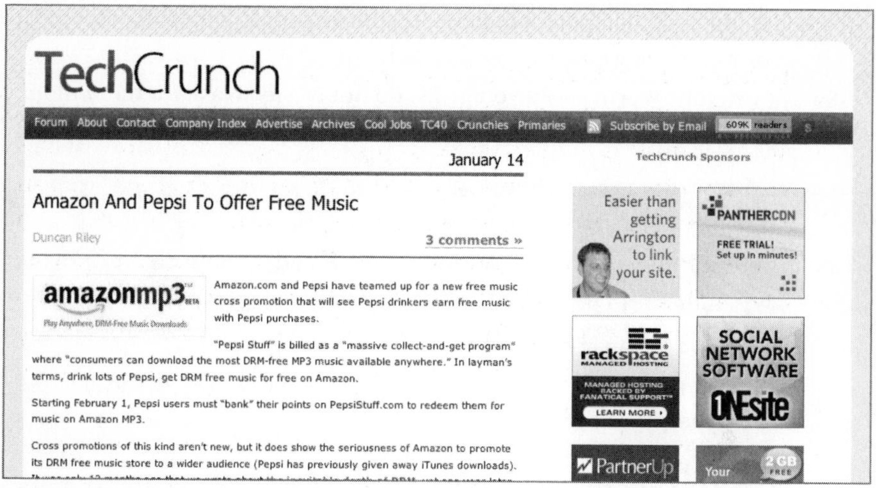

**Figure 9-1:** www.techcrunch.com

According to Wikipedia, TechCrunch was launched in 2005, and when the previous edition of this book was written it was claimed they made a total of $200,000 a *month* in revenue. Now with over three million regular readers, I am sure that has increased even despite the global advertising downturn. Advertisers benefit from both the massive amount of traffic the blog generates and awareness from the specific target audience.

Scoops made TechCrunch the draw that it is now. Having a direct line to insider gossip means they break the news and everyone else has to follow. This is vital for a news site, in terms of building authority and credibility. Opinions are great, but people universally sit up and take notice of big news that affects their industry.

You could say TechCrunch can base its success on getting to the news first, but it also benefits from a self-fulfilling cycle; everyone reads TechCrunch, so people come to them with stories, which get lots of coverage, which means everyone reads TechCrunch!

In addition to the blogs, TechCrunch also launched TechCrunch20, a conference that showcases startups and their products and services — yet another way they build awareness, credibility, and revenue.

## Lessons from TechCrunch

1. **Break news** — Get news early, and post it fast.
2. **Network** — Get to know all the movers and shakers in your niche.

3. **Get big** — Scale matters in news; the more people with their ears to the ground, the more news you can dish out.
4. **Know your worth** — As you grow, do not be shy to ask for more money from advertisers.

---

**EXERCISE**

Log in to the Problogger Book Member Download Area to catch up with more case studies and interviews with successful bloggers:

`http://probloggerbook.com/bonus/`

If you have not already, sign up here: (Make sure you type the address exactly as shown.)

`http://probloggerbook.com/?/register/bonus`

---

## Scobleizer

Robert Scoble is one of the most well-known veteran bloggers and probably the best example I can give of an employee blogger. Although he has his own popular Scobleizer blog (Figure 9-2), his earnings mainly come from the people who employ him as a blogging personality.

Most people first heard of Robert when he worked for Microsoft as an evangelist. His most recent gig is working with the web hosting company, Rackspace.

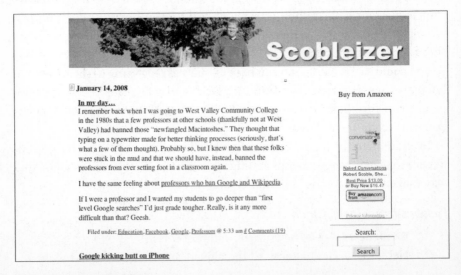

**Figure 9-2:** http://scobleizer.com

His claim to fame is his connections; he seems to know all the big names personally. This powerful address book has been at the core of his blogging career, especially with his videos in which he goes out and interviews interesting people from the industry.

While obviously he makes most use of his high-profile connections, he is a massive networker online too, having a massive following on Twitter and a huge number of Facebook friends.

### Lessons from Robert Scoble

1. **Network** — Be a hub and a connector. Robert seems to spend as much time having lunches with movers and shakers as he does blogging and speaking. Blogging is as much about relationships as it is writing. To succeed, you need great content, of course, but it also helps to be well connected.

2. **Links should be unique and interesting** — Link to great stuff that others haven't noticed. One of the great things about Robert's link blog is that it doesn't just replicate the popular Digg and del.icio.us stories — he has his own sources. If you are linking out to the same old stuff, people won't need your feed cluttering up their reader. Find fresh and exciting new stuff, though, and your readers will reward you.

3. **Nobody is perfect** — Many bloggers try to project an image of perfection. Admit when you are wrong; there is no harm in it. In fact, it could do you a world of good. I believe part of Robert's success in helping Microsoft repair its relationship with the public was Robert's willingness to admit when mistakes had been made, personally or by the company. This builds trust.

4. **Little and often** — Some days Scoble posts a lot. Darren has commented a couple of times about the dangers of misjudging posting frequency. Some readers are put off by too much content too fast. I believe why it works for Robert is he posts little and often. Small, bite-sized, 15-second posts work well.

### EXERCISE

Robert Scoble owes a large part of his success to his huge network of contacts. Make a plan for how you are going to grow your network starting today.

## Four-Hour Work Week

Tim Ferriss exploded onto the scene in 2007, seemingly from nowhere. His impact was due to a killer blog (Figure 9-3) and book-launch combination. Both the blog and book mutually fueled the buzz, meaning at the time there were few bloggers who hadn't at least heard about him.

### Lessons from Tim Ferriss

1. **Craft your posts** — Unlike many of the blogs listed here, Tim does not post several times a day. In fact, there can be several days between posts. He explained in a ProBlogger interview that this allows him to more carefully craft his articles and tweak his headlines; it also allows time for comments to accumulate.

2. **Say what you mean** — Some of his posts are intentionally controversial. He says top stories almost always polarize people, so he tries to take a strong stand on one side or the other of an issue.

3. **Cover topics that anyone can comment on** — Tim suggests considering subjects that he can imagine allowing his parents, siblings, or friends having advice to share.

**Figure 9-3:** www.thefourhourworkweek.com/blog

## PopCrunch

No relation to TechCrunch, PopCrunch (Figure 9-4) is a blog in the super-competitive celebrity niche, bringing all the celebrity gossip like an online version of the celebrity magazines you see in the supermarket newsstands.

**Figure 9-4:** www.popcrunch.com

The key to PopCrunch, just like TechCrunch, is getting the story out first. Revenue for the blog all comes from leveraging its traffic with advertising. Whereas other blogs use traffic as a draw for advertisers along with branding and reputation benefits, PopCrunch, in the main, sells impression-based CPM ads, meaning the more page views it gets, the more money it makes. It pays off because it clears a good five-figure income each and every month, and much more when it manages to scoop a big story.

As you can imagine, PopCrunch uses every traffic trick in the book, from SEO through to really working the social media sites. Recently it has been experimenting with video, creating PopCrunch TV.

Learning the scale lessons of TechCrunch, Ryan Caldwell, PopCrunch's founder, prides himself on putting every cent of revenue back into the blog in order to grow.

## *Lessons from PopCrunch*

1. **Learn and implement** — Do your research; find out what works; use what you learn from other niches in your own.
2. **Mix media** — Try video, try audio; see what your audience reacts to.
3. **Promote** — Yes, content is king, but who will notice without the traffic? Push the traffic any way you can. Only when you really reach the top can you stop promoting completely.

---

**EXERCISE**

Look around your niche and your favorite blogs. Can you do the same exercise and learn something from each of them?

---

# Summary

Looking at the various writing styles, promotion tactics, and ways people approach earning from their blogging, you can tell there is an approach out there to suit anybody. We have seen a famous employee blogger, bloggers who write books, people who earn from advertising, and those who make money from courses. It is clear there is no single "right way"; success is limited only by your imagination.

Though you can derive a great deal of pleasure from the activity of blogging, for most people blogging is a means to an end. As you have seen in this chapter, how you approach it can be as diverse as the people who take part. We hope you can find some ideas and inspiration from these successful bloggers' stories.

# 10 Creating Something Worthwhile

So you have started a blog. You want to make money or you have some other goal in mind. You are in it for yourself. This is all well and good, but to actually achieve those goals, you will have to gather readers, build traffic, network, and build links. Basically, to achieve your goals you are going to have to serve an audience.

What does "serving an audience" mean? Rather than prioritize your advertising, affiliates, and sales, you have to give readers what they want. It means making something useful, something that people will want to talk about (favorably).

This is the real trick, the difference between winning and losing, and the subject of this chapter.

## Know Your Audience

Before you can serve an audience, you need to know who they are! You need to really understand your readers, both through research and planning before you launch, and after you launch through talking to them.

If you are already a member of the community in which you are working, you will have an advantage here; however, you still need to consider who your target readers will be and what they would like to see. Consider the following:

- What are they called?
- Who do they think they are?
- Who are they really?
- Who do they want to be?
- Who do they like?
- Who don't they like?

- Who is their peer group?
- Who do they not identify with?
- What are their beliefs?
- Where do they live?
- Where do they work?
- Where do they learn?
- Where do they want to be?
- What are their needs?
- How old are they?
- How youthful do they act?
- How conservative are they?
- What are their driving ambitions?
- What are their wants and needs?
- What are their pleasures?
- What are their pains?
- What do they love?
- What do they hate?

To really appeal to an audience, you have to go beyond "nice," "ok," and "good enough." Ask yourself how you can take your blog to the next level, to be not just merely adequate but must-have. Not just interesting, but *compelling*.

> **EXERCISE**
>
> Create pen portraits for your reader group. Write down everything you know about them. Once you have a good idea of who you are targeting, try to brainstorm content ideas that they would absolutely *love*.

## Being Remarkable

Thanks to Seth Godin and his books, in particular *Purple Cow*, many bloggers know and understand the need to be "remarkable." Remarkable is what makes ideas spread. The problem is that being aware of the need is not the same as putting it into practice. Take these points for example:

- **Attention is not compelling** — Stripping naked or shouting "fire" gets you noticed but is not valuable. Forget attention seeking and create value.

- **Be radical** — Half-measures won't do. People only remember the biggest, fastest, richest, easiest, hardest, most expensive, cheapest, and whatever superlative you can think of.
- **It's not fashion** — Fashion is fleeting. It is following a bandwagon; if it is already being talked about you are already too late.

  It's not about *you*. This is about your reader; leave your ego out of it. One of the biggest mistakes bloggers make is being all me-me-me.
- **People should care** — If people do not love it or hate it, then you need to push harder. "Like" is not remarkable; it should cause passion.

If you manage to make something remarkable, your task of spreading your message and promoting your blog will be so much easier. A successful blog is all about having your brand spread far and wide.

### EXERCISE

Seth Godin tells us to look out for "Purple Cows." Think of things in your life that are remarkable. What lifts them above being "average," "normal," or "nice"?

# What Causes Ideas to Spread?

If you think about the last time you told someone something you heard, it will likely have been the following:

- **Different/New** — People do not talk about things that are usual and ordinary. People take notice of things that are new or different. English Cut (Figure 10-1) was the first blog about men's suits anyone had heard of; start a blog like that today, and nobody would take notice.
- **Newsworthy** — News is probably the biggest type of information to spread, but that doesn't always mean it is new or different. In some cases it is the nature of the story that helps it spread. Sometimes ordinary things can become news if they happen to someone important.
- **Easy to understand** — If you have to puzzle over something before you get it, it will in most cases seem like too much effort, even if you think it is important in some way. Simplify your message, and it will spread more effectively.

**Figure 10-1:** www.englishcut.com

- **Easy to remember** — How will people spread your ideas if they can't remember them? It's just like jokes; some of us have a talent for remembering and telling them, but even though I love to listen to comedians tell complex stories, I can recall and retell only the most basic.
- **Easy to communicate** — There is a good reason why politicians use sound bites; they are easy to remember and communicate. Make it easy to get the point across. Provide "send to friend" and bookmarking features.
- **Beneficial** — Will your story help someone? Will it make them laugh? What will the sender and recipient gain? The more beneficial, the more it will spread; self-interest almost always comes into play.

## EXERCISE

For a week, make a mental note of every piece of news and gossip you come across. Try to determine how the piece of information was transmitted to you and which you take note of or share, and which "wither on the vine."

# Making Your Blog Useful

Useful blogs can be difficult to define, but we can all spot one. Spend any meaningful time in the company of a blog-reading tool, and we become masters at it. We decide the fate of a feed in an instant sometimes, like cruel judges on some reality-TV talent contest. But the question is: What defines those blogs that make it? Why are some blogs useful and others a waste of time?

Ask yourself what your favorite blogs have in common. Think of your absolute, number-one, favorite blog in the world. For Darren it is Lifehacker. For me, it is Scott Adams' Dilbert blog.

Why do you like the blog that you've identified? What keeps you going back so often?

Scott Adams is an incredibly witty guy, but he also makes me think. I go to his blog as escape, to think about something other than work. With Lifehacker there are a few things Darren enjoys, but the main factor is that it's a blog that regularly provides life-enhancing tips.

## Useful-Blog Properties

We will all have different answers, but if we gathered the properties of those favorite blogs together, I expect we could group the answers into one or more of the following categories:

- **Entertaining** — Blogs are increasingly being used as entertainment. People are going to them for laughs, for gossip, and for fun conversation.
- **Educational** — Some blog readers are primarily interested in learning something new about a given topic.
- **Informative** — Many successful blogs are built on the thirst that some have to be informed on an issue, product, or topic.
- **Thoughtful** — Some blog readers want a place where they can have their minds open to viewpoints, and have a good old-fashioned dialogue, debate, or even a fight over an issue.
- **Breaking news** — Many blog readers just want to be kept up-to-date in a field.
- **Community** — Some very successful blogs tap into the need that people have to connect and belong. Quite often the topic is secondary to these connections.

Each blog has the potential to be "useful," and each successful blog will approach it in its own way, perhaps using a combination of the preceding factors.

Now think about your current or planned blog; which of the previous properties can you provide?

---

**PROBLOGGER BLOG TIP: THE ULTIMATE GOAL**

Creating a blog that people absolutely cannot live without is a rare thing indeed, but should be your goal. If you do not strive to make your blog the best it can be, it will be easy to slip into "good enough" and then on toward mediocrity. Always be thinking, "How can I make this better?"

---

## Creating Useful Content Today

Whether you have an existing blog or want to get started today, read through the following tips and implement them right away.

### Add Value

Don't just report the same news that everyone else is reporting; add value to it by expressing your opinion, analyzing it, helping readers interpret it, and so on. If your blog is a "newsy"-type blog, the next time you write a post, take a moment before hitting "Publish" to ask yourself if you've added anything to the story. Tell your readers what you think, make a comment about how it applies to you (or might apply to others), look back and identify patterns in the story, or look forward and make a prediction about where things might be headed. Though some people do want to hear the latest news, they'll become loyal to you as a news source if you help them make sense of it.

### Ask Questions

Asking questions brings you closer to your readers and gives you insight into how they think. This works better on some blogs than others (the topic and reader numbers come into play), but a real question for readers is a great starting place for useful content. I love to ask questions on my blog, and I try to do it regularly (see Figure 10-2).

**Do You Block Ads?**
- Yes most of them, but I don't consider them evil. I just don't click them anyway so I prefer clean sites[1]
  63
- No, ad blockers are selfish
  59
- No, but I can't argue with someone who chooses to block them for their own reason.[1]
  22
- Yes, ads are evil
  21
- I block popups only but can't argue with someone trying to block all ads[1]
  20
- Block popups and banner ads[1]
  18
- Who or what are ad blockers?
  11
- Undecided
  5
- Yes, I hate all forms of commercial web
  4
- Only Flash Ads[1]
  3
- I unblock ads on sites I want to support.[1]
  3

**Figure 10-2:** An example poll.

## Mine Your Feedback

Your comments and inbox are rich sources of relevant material and burning questions. If readers take time to ask you a question, you know it matters to them — and more than likely to many of your other readers also.

**PROBLOGGER BLOG TIP: STEAL FEEDBACK**

Read blog comments and forum messages in your niche and take a note of good questions and suggestions! Using feedback doesn't have to be restricted to messages sent to you directly.

## Tell Your Story

Telling *your* stories can be very powerful. Put yourself into your posts; talk about how you learned what you are talking about. Give examples, be humorous, and express emotion. Readers want to connect with you, and telling a story rather than "just the facts" helps bring alive the topic.

> **EXERCISE**
>
> What stories do you have to tell? What are the lessons you learned? Next time you are relating a story that you think is interesting, make a note of it for use in your blog.

## Entertain

Be humorous, intriguing, irreverent, fun, push boundaries, surprise your readers, include a little spice. Use entertaining pictures, video, audio, and so on. Be playful.

## Inform

Produce "how to" or "tips" posts. You might also want to do "introduction to…"-type posts. Ask readers what they want to learn about and then answer their questions.

## Build Community

Write inspirational posts with heart. Pay a lot of attention to the readers you have, ask lots of questions, answer their questions; empower people to contribute as much as they can. Include everyone; do not fall into the trap of "in" jokes and shorthand. Warmth, welcoming, and discussion are the keys to a great community.

> **EXERCISE**
>
> When was the last time you felt welcomed into a community? When did you feel unwelcome or even hostility? What did the community members do differently in each case? Can you implement any of those positive factors into your blog?

Each blog will have a different mix of goals and objectives. You might like to attempt to achieve more than one of the above, but the key is to know what exactly you're aiming for!

# Summary

The most critical aspect of all this is to put your audience first and do it in a new and original way. As time goes on, standing out among the crowd is going to get harder and harder. You need to find a way to better serve readers while covering new ground.

Aim to be unique, remarkable, compelling, and most of all, useful, and your blog will have success long after many other bloggers have given up.

# 11 Taking Your Blog to the Next Level: A Case Study

Much of what we've covered so far focuses upon the introductory stages of blogging, but what happens when your blog has been around for a while and you want to take it up to the next level?

How do you expand it from being just another blog that has a few readers and makes a part time income to being a profitable business in and of itself?

In this chapter I walk you through the way that I've grown my Digital Photography School (DPS) blog into a blog that is read by over 3 million visitors a month and which has sent blog buyers my way with seven-figure offers.

## The Launch of DPS — Years 1-2

On a rainy afternoon in April 2006 I received another email from a reader of my existing camera review blog asking for advice on how they should use their camera in low-light situations.

I'd been developing a small blog that aggregated camera reviews from around the Web for a couple of years now, and emails asking for advice on how to use cameras was a pretty regular thing to hit my inbox. I'd only ever written camera review posts and avoided "how to" content on my existing photography blog and usually replied to these requests for help with a "sorry but I don't write that type of post" email.

On this day I was about to send this type of reply when on a whim I decided to write a short tutorial on how to use a camera in low-light situations. After completing the post I was about to publish it on my review blog when an idea struck me: What if I started a new "how to" photography blog?

Without a lot of thought I registered www.digital-photography-school.com (something I wish I'd put a little more thought into as it is quite a mouthful), found a free template, added the first post and launched the blog.

Over the next few days and before promoting the new blog anywhere, I wrote another few posts so that the blog would have a few articles to read. I then linked to it from my existing review blog and it was launched.

That first week or so the blog had around 200 visitors and made less than a dollar via AdSense.

## Building Foundations

My strategy with DPS was always to approach the first two years of the blog as a "launch phase." My hope was to spend the initial year or two focusing upon a number of foundational activities that I believed would ensure that blog reached its potential in later years. Here's what I spent most of my time on in the first year:

### Foundation 1: Content

For a book about making money from blogs, this book has spent a lot of time on the topic of "content." The reason for this is that both Chris and I firmly believe that for a blog to be successful it needs to be useful to readers through providing content that solves their problems and meets their needs.

As a result the first year of DPS was all about identifying the type of problems that beginner photographers have and writing posts that provided them with solutions. These days the blog covers a wider array of topics and levels.

During the first two years of DPS I wrote 95% of the content on the site. I did occasionally attract other guest posts from photographers from other sites, but the bulk of it was an in-house activity. This was partly because I am a bit of a control freak and wanted to ensure that the quality was high, but also it was something I did while the income of the site grew to the point where we could hire staff writers.

### Foundation 2: Promotion

I utilized many of the techniques covered in Chapter 7 of this book in building my readership. Networking with other bloggers, optimizing the blog for Search Engines, and writing content for social media type sites like Digg and StumbleUpon were all very important in the early days.

In addition to this I also asked myself two important questions:

- Who do I want to read my blog?
- Where do these people already gather online?

These are crucial questions for any blogger to ask — if you can identify who your potential readers are and then find where they're gathering in numbers online, then you have some great places to start when promoting your blog.

For me the answer to question number 1 was simply "beginner photographers."

Knowing this helped me to identify their gathering points, which included the following:

- Photosharing such as Flickr, where I started to hang out more and started a "group" to attract readers
- Other photography blogs and sites, where I began to write a few guest posts and network with site owners
- Photography forums, where I became more active
- Blogs on related topics; for example, I began to submit stories to Lifehacker, a blog with a broader topic than DPS but that linked to us numerous times.

After I identified several gathering points for potential readers, I worked hard on being a genuine and useful member and contributor of these sites. This, in time, drew people to check out who I was and what my site was about.

### Foundation 3: Community

When I started DPS it didn't have any kind of community at all. In fact when I started the blog it wasn't set up to enable readers to leave comments (a bit of an experiment to see how it would go).

Although I did leave comments switched off for a few months, I did move towards adding several community elements to the site in the first year, including starting a Flickr group that enabled readers to interact and share photos. I also ran some competitions.

When I did switch on comments, I also began regularly to ask readers questions, run polls, have debates, and give readers opportunities to share photos.

Also after around six months, I added a new forum area to the site. I used vBulletin as the forum platform and started it with a small number of discussion areas. I quickly found a number of forum members to help me moderate the forum on a voluntary basis. This forum area has grown to well over 80,000 members and is a thriving part of DPS today.

### Foundation 4: Capturing Contacts

Perhaps the most important thing I did from the very first month of DPS was to start a weekly email newsletter. This started after a family member asked how they could find out about new articles on the site. I explained that they could subscribe to my RSS feed; their blank face made me realize that many people have no idea what RSS is or how to use it.

Email is a far more familiar technology for most people so I started a newsletter and invited readers to subscribe and give me permission to email them once a week with the site's latest tips, tutorials, reviews, and offers. To this day over a quarter of a million subscribers are newsletter subscribers.

I will describe how I use these emails to drive traffic, build community, and make money later in this chapter.

## Monetization

In the first two years my primary focus was creating quality content, promoting my blog, building a community, and capturing contacts with my newsletter.

Making money from the site was not my primary concern in this phase; however, I didn't ignore it completely. From day one the site was monetized through two primary means:

- **Advertising** — I've always run AdSense and Chitika ad network ads on this site. While these networks don't convert brilliantly in some niches, they outperformed other monetization strategies in the early days of the site as I built a readership.

  In time and as reader numbers grew we've also begun to attract more direct advertisers and sponsors for the site. This is slowly starting to replace the ad network ads which now fill in remnant and unsold ad units.

- **Affiliate Promotions** — As a secondary income stream, I've done some affiliate marketing. Initially I restricted marketing to promotions of cameras, other photography products, and books on Amazon, but towards the end of our second year, we started to promote other people's photography training courses.

# Consolidation and Expansion — Year 3-4

During the first two years of DPS our readership grew considerably. My focus upon providing useful content, heavily promoting it, and then capturing those new readers with our newsletter and forum worked well, and the site grew to around 25,000 visitors a day. It finally began making enough money for me to consider expanding the site.

Over the course of the next couple of years, we added staff writers, expanded topics, updated our site design, expanded our use of social media, and more.

## Staff Writers

After the site became profitable, I began to advertise for paid contributors to the site. I did this with a simple ad on the ProBlogger job boards and quickly had more qualified applicants than I could use. I settled on 5 weekly contributors to supplement my own articles.

Over the last year I grew this writing team from 5 to 10; when some moved on I hired others. I also formed a secondary group of guest writers who occasionally submit content on a voluntary basis. These guests are either readers who want to help the community or are photographers from other sites who want to grow their profile.

## Expansion of Topics

Initially DPS unashamedly was all about beginner photographers and focused solely upon writing tips on how to use cameras. After we grew our readership to a point where things were very solid, I made the decision to expand the site to include two new areas: post production (how to use Photoshop and other software), and camera reviews.

This expansion grew largely out of readers asking questions about these topics in our forum as well as the suspicion that I had that they would be profitable areas. The camera review area is particularly profitable due to affiliate promotion on Amazon and the fact that cameras are a bigger ticket item and lead to healthy commissions.

As part of this expansion (and the hiring of extra writers) I've now increased the posting frequency on DPS from once per day to two articles per day (which also helped grow traffic to the site).

## New Design

DPS has had three designs since its launch. When I started it, I launched with a free template that I tweaked to make it a little more unique. Twelve months in, I hired a designer to come up with a more professional site design, but the site quickly outgrew that look and layout.

Late in 2008, I hired Matt Brett to give DPS a complete overhaul. This design made way for the expansion in topics, integrated the forum and blog a little better, and promoted multiple page views for first-time visitors to the site, which led to the better capturing of new readers to our newsletter.

Such custom designs are certainly not cheap, but often lead to a noticeable increase in page views. They also give first-time visitors and potential advertisers and other key influencers in a niche a good first impression of your blog.

## Social Media

I have always been intentional about developing a social media presence with DPS since its launch. However there has been a real shift in how I've done this in the last two years.

Early on, the focus was much more about writing content for social bookmarking sites like Digg, Delicious, and StumbleUpon. While DPS still receives decent traffic from social bookmarking sites, I focus less upon targeting these sites today.

Instead I am much happier to let our community submit our content to these sites as they wish and focus more upon building a presence on social networking sites like Twitter and Facebook, where we have DPS specific accounts and pages.

## Increased Focus upon Affiliate Marketing

During the third year of DPS the global financial crisis began. As I began to see the economy failing, I realized that relying so heavily upon advertising as a revenue stream was not a good move. I decided to diversify my income.

One diversification strategy was to focus more upon promoting products with affiliate marketing. I began to seek out existing affiliate programs in the photography space to promote. At that time, not many existed although I did find a couple of e-books and training courses that I promoted heavily with good results.

The problem I faced was that after I'd promoted these resources to readers once or twice, conversions dropped drastically as readers would either buy the product or decide not to. I needed more products to promote.

I had exhausted existing quality products to promote, so I began to approach others who were selling photography products without having affiliate programs to see if they'd be interested in starting affiliate programs for us. I was surprised to find that almost everyone I approached said yes and started up affiliate programs for us to use.

As a result, our affiliate marketing grew from about 10% of our revenue to around 35% of it in a year, more than making up for the slump in advertising revenue (which turned out to be not as bad as I'd anticipated).

## DPS Resources

The other diversification strategy that I worked on in the fourth year was to begin developing our very own product — an e-book on Portrait Photography entitled "The Essential Guide to Portrait Photography."

The e-book was a collection of edited and updated posts from the DPS blog on the topic of portraits. It also was bundled with a series of interviews from professional photographers sharing their tips on portraiture.

The e-book, which we launched in November of 2009, was around 80 pages long and packed full of information. It was professionally designed and proofread. It sold at $19.95 USD (discounted by 25% in launch week) and during it's first week of sales generated over $70,000 USD in income.

Sales continue at a rate of 10-30 copies per day and so this first e-book continues to be a worthwhile revenue stream even months after its initial release.

E-books and other photography resources will continue to be a growing focus for DPS moving forward. The site continues to sell advertising and engage in affiliate marketing but numerous other e-books are currently at different stages of production and will launch in the coming year.

## DPS Today

Digital Photography School is certainly not the largest or most profitable blog in the blogosphere today. In many ways I look at it and see a relatively young blog that can be expanded in numerous ways.

However, it has grown from a blog with a handful of weekly readers making less than a dollar a week into one that is read by over 3 million readers a month and that generates several hundred thousand dollars in revenue a year.

The following sections describe how I manage the DPS blog today.

# Using Email to Drive Traffic and Make Money

Email newsletters are a central strategy in the development of DPS. Ever since launch I've offered readers the option of subscribing to receive updates from the site via a simple weekly newsletter that gives them links to new content on the site and hot discussions in the forum.

The benefits of this newsletter to DPS are numerous:

- It drives significant traffic each week to the site. Newsletter days are always our biggest days.
- It makes money. I sell advertising space to advertisers, launch our own products, and run affiliate promotions through the newsletters I send.
- It builds community. Newsletters can be used to build community moral, launch competitions, and direct people to interactive areas on the site.
- It's great for branding. Having a weekly point of contact with readers reinforces our brand and builds reader loyalty.

Firstly a word about technology, I use Aweber (Aweber.com) to deliver my emails. However, many email newsletter services are avaible, and you can use any one that allows you to set up an auto-responder or sequence of emails.

> **NOTE**
>
> The process I'm about to share started out very very simple and has slowly developed with time. In fact it continues to develop as I learn more, and by no means is where I want to take it.... *yet.*

Lets start with a visual on how my process looks before I explain the elements:

If you'd like to subscribe to the newsletter to experience it firsthand, you can do so at `http://bit.ly/subscribeDPS`.

## Getting the Readers to Subscribe

Because email newsletters are such an important part of my site, I put a lot of emphasis upon getting this conversion moment with those who visit. There are a variety of places around the blog where I attempt to get readers to sign up. Some are subtle (including in sidebars), and others are not (including a pop-up signup box that readers see 20-30 seconds after they arrive on the blog).

The pop-up is set to show only once per visitor (unless they're blocking cookies), and although it is intrusive and I was very hesitant about adding it, it has been incredibly effective at getting readers to sign up. Before I started using pop-ups I averaged 40 confirmed subscribers a day. After adding the pop-up, I averaged 350 per day. (This is now well over 500 subscribers a day.)

The pop-up does annoy a handful of readers. (I get an email or two per month with a complaint about it.) However, because of the payoff, it's something I've decided to continue.

## Sending a Welcome Email

When a new subscriber signs up and confirms their subscription (via email), a welcome email goes out immediately. This email is all about making them feel good about subscribing and giving them a quick introduction to the site.

I'm presuming that most people who sign up for the newsletter are new to the site, so it's a great opportunity to introduce myself, show them around and help get their expectations right about the site.

This welcome email has a site logo, my picture, some links to key parts of the site like the forum, some suggested reading for catching up on key posts in our archives, and some information about what the subscriber will receive in the coming weeks in terms of future emails.

The email also asks people to add the email address that emails are sent from to their white list/contact list to help ensure emails are delivered.

This welcome is written in a personal and friendly style and seems to connect as I get a lot of replies to this email from new subscribers thanking me for the personal welcome.

## Providing Weekly Updates

Weekly updates are what readers get the most. They're largely updates on what has happened on the blog/forums in the past week.

I usually have the following sections in these weekly updates:

- **Welcome** — Usually, this is just a sentence that introduces the week. If there's something important in the newsletter, I highlight it here. Sometimes I also offer a quick update on something cool that happened on the site during the week (record day of traffic, milestone in terms of subscribers, a mention in the press). This kind of update seems to build morale/momentum among readers.

- **Quick Links** — Here I share the weekly assignment, any discussion oriented posts/polls, any competition announcements, and occasionally a "featured post" that I want to push traffic to.
- **Tips, Tutorials, and Techniques** — This includes new blog posts of a more general nature.
- **Recommended Resource** — Most often this is an affiliate promotion (a great product), but occasionally this section functions as a message from our sponsors , which is a sold-ad position.
- **Post Production Tips** — Here I include updates from this section of the blog.
- **New Gear, Tips, and Reviews** — Again, I offer updates from this section of the blog.
- **Hot Forum Threads** — This consists of a bit of a summary of key threads happening in the forum.

Although the previous list provides a basic newsletter template, I do mix things up a bit. Some weeks I run a little promotion of our Twitter or Facebook accounts. Other weeks, I might throw in some older posts from the archives, and sometimes I run a promotion encouraging readers to forward the email to a friend. Really, anything can go in these emails as long as they're on topic and useful.

Keep in mind the main goals of these weekly updates:

- Drive traffic to the site.
- Build community, reinforce brand with readers.
- Make money through the promotions.

Readers love these newsletters because although they're largely links to the site, the links are all content rich and useful resources. I title these emails "Photography Tips for Your Weekend" and that's how many of our readers use them — as a spring board into their weekend with their cameras.

**NOTE**

I put together these emails manually. They take me an hour or two a week to do. There are tools that send out automated update emails (Aweber has one) but I prefer to do it manually to ensure that the emails are tailored for maximum impact and usefulness.

## *Providing Themed Updates*

Themed updates are all about sending readers back to old but useful content around a single theme.

The idea came about when I realized that new readers of my blog, were not seeing the majority of my blogs' thousands of pages of content. Although I occasionally link back to key posts, most of my archives don't get a lot of traffic.

Here's how my themed updates work.

I use the auto responder or followup feature of Aweber to set up these emails. This means that they go out at pre-determined intervals to readers a certain number of days after their last scheduled email.

1. The first email in the sequence is the previously mentioned welcome email.
2. Thirty days after the welcome email, the subscriber receives the first "themed" email. The topic is "Exposure" and is a newsletter that contains a short intro to the topic of how to get good exposure in photography and then some links back to some of our most useful tutorials on that topic. It also recommends some good books on exposure (with affiliate links).
3. Thirty days after the Exposure email, subscribers get another themed email about composition that contains links to some of our best posts on that topic. (Remember they're getting weekly updates in between.) It also recommends good books on the topic (with affiliate links to Amazon).
4. Thirty days later subscribers get an email on portraiture (same format as the previous one with links to archive posts and books). Thirty days later they get another themed email (and so on).

The main goals of these "themed updates" are as follows:

- Drive traffic to the site, particularly older posts.
- Make money through the affiliate links. Although they're not big ticket items, they do convert.

These emails do take some time to set up but once they're set up they become automated and go out every day without me ever having to think about them. With 500+ people signing up for my newsletter every day I know that

500 people are getting each of these emails on a daily basis. I have six of these emails set up in a sequence at present and add more to the list every now and again, so I know 3000 people in total get them each day of the week — forever. This is a set and forget traffic generator!

### Sending Promotional Emails

This is the most recent addition to my sequence of emails and I'm still perfecting their use, but the signs are very promising already.

I use the auto-responder sequence mentioned previously to deliver these. (They're going to go out every month or two.) The content of these emails highlights a resource or product that I recommend to readers.

The products are either my own product or affiliate products that I take a commission from any sale of. We disclose that relationship in the email and get a lot of positive feedback from readers on the disclosure.

The key to these promotional emails is to choose products that you genuinely recommend (or to develop your own great product). The reason for this is that at any point subscribers can leave your list. And they will. If you push too hard or recommend dodgy products they can leave (with a bad taste in their mouth).

The first of these "promotional" emails in our sequence goes out 8 days after someone signs up to our newsletter. (This ensures tht they get at least one of our weekly updates first.) The email simply reinforces my previous welcome to the list and offers the reader a 25% off discount on our Portraits E-book letting them know that we've previously offered all readers the chance at this discount and wanted to extend it to them also for a limited time.

This is a low pressure sell and a short email. It simply makes the offer and then backs off to let the person make their decision.

The second promotional email goes out a couple of months later and is for a high quality photography training course. Again it's a low pressure sell — no hype, no obligations. We simply make a genuine recommendation and let people make up their minds.

Promotional emails are a new addition to my email sequence but I'm already seeing great conversions.

The main goal of these promotional updates is  to make money through sales and affiliate promotions. The money these emails earn starts with a bang when you send it out to the bulk of your list on the first day, but after that it becomes a steady trickle. Keep in mind that once you have a number of these emails set up in your sequence you can be having a number of promotions paying off each day.

## Concluding Thoughts on the DPS Email Sequence

This mix of emails gets very positive results. I work hard to keep them a win/win for our readers and our blog by providing useful and relevant information and generating income. So far I think I've got the balance right. I regularly get emails from readers saying thanks for the newsletter, and if I'm even an hour or two late sending it, I get emails asking where it is. On a revenue front, it's increasingly profitable; between the sales of products and the ad revenue increases from the increased traffic, it certainly has become a central part of my income stream to have this email list.

With the cycle as it is, readers do occasionally get two emails in a week. However it's never more than that and on most weeks, it is just the one weekly email. I make it clear when they sign up that it's at least weekly, to get this expectation right, as I don't want them feeling duped into signing up.

I also use Aweber's scheduling feature for the auto responder emails, which allows me to specify what days of the week they can go out. I schedule the sequenced emails (the themed and promotional ones) so that they never go out on a Thursday or Friday (the same day as the weekly ones).

## Summary

It can be easy to make the mistake of coming across an established blog and thinking that it has always been the way that you see it today. My hope is that this case study will not only illustrate some of the techniques and strategies for building successful blogs that Chris and I have spoken about in this book, but that it will also illustrate how blogs evolve and grow over time.

# Index